D1570137

The Birds
of Konza

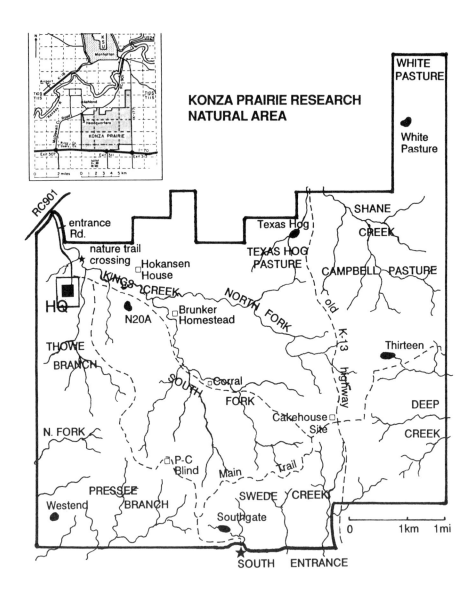

KONZA PRAIRIE RESEARCH
NATURAL AREA

The Birds of Konza

THE AVIAN ECOLOGY
OF THE TALLGRASS PRAIRIE

John L. Zimmerman

University Press of Kansas

Photograph of common poorwill is by James Holloway; all others are by David Rintoul.

Published by the University Press of Kansas (Lawrence, Kansas 66049), which was organized by the Kansas Board of Regents and is operated and funded by Emporia State University, Fort Hays State University, Kansas State University, Pittsburg State University, the University of Kansas, and Wichita State University

Library of Congress Cataloging-in-Publication Data

Zimmerman, John L., 1933–
    The birds of Konza : the avian ecology of the tallgrass prairie /
John L. Zimmerman.
        p. cm.
    Includes bibliographical references (p.   ) and index.
    ISBN 0-7006-0597-5 (hardcover)
    1. Birds—Kansas—Konza Prairie Research Natural Area—Ecology.
    2. Birds—Kansas—Konza Prairie Research Natural Area—Migration.
    3. Birds—Kansas—Konza Prairie Research Natural Area. I. Title.
QL684.K2Z545   1993
598.252′643′0978129—dc20   92-42414

British Library Cataloguing in Publication Data is available.

Printed in the United States of America
10 9 8 7 6 5 4 3 2 1

The paper used in this publication meets the minimum requirements of the American National Standard for Permanence of Paper for Printed Library Materials Z39.48-1984.

Contents

CONTENTS

Tables and Figures

Preface

The natural history and ecology of bird species that occur in tall-grass prairies have been described, but often these accounts have been based on studies conducted with more easterly populations. Since the Great Plains is the meeting ground between East and West, distributions and evolution of several prairie species have been the focus of exemplary analyses discussed in major ornithological texts. One of the more successful components of the International Biological Program during the third quarter of this century was a description and quantification of grassland ecosystems, including that of the tallgrass prairie. The role of birds in ecosystem process was an essential segment of this endeavor. There have also been short-term studies of prairie bird communities, some simply descriptive but others relating community structure to factors in the environment that might affect the composition of the community. However, these studies were largely limited to the grassland community, excluding other communities integral to the characteristic patterns of the tallgrass prairie.

Because of biases based on an understanding developed from studies of nonprairie populations of grassland birds and an understanding of "prairie" based on studies limited to the grassland community or one component of its functional processes, there is little appreciation of prairie bird populations within the context of the total landscape of the tallgrass prairie region. It may come as a surprise to some, for example, to learn that the

American tree sparrow is the most abundant species during winter on tallgrass prairie or that breeding brown-headed cowbirds are neither monogamous nor territorial. This most mesic of all grasslands is a heterogeneous panorama that involves variously sized patches of grass, forb, and woody vegetation developed across a terrain of different exposures and water availabilities and existing in a midcontinental climate characterized by extremes. Both primevally and as a result of human husbandry, this mosaic is overlain by the variable impacts imposed by grazing and periodic fires.

The Flint Hills Upland is a 70-kilometer(km)-wide band extending north and south astride the 97th meridian across Kansas. This range of hills is an eastward-facing, dissected escarpment of resistant limestones that form benches between intervening slopes of shale. The terrain has been a deterrent to cultivation; hence the Flint Hills remain covered by extensive tracts of virgin tallgrass prairie, at least in the uplands. The Konza Prairie Research Natural Area is a 3,486-hectare (ha) ecological reserve in the northern Flint Hills (Riley and Geary counties), purchased by the Nature Conservancy between 1971 and 1979 and administered by the Division of Biology at Kansas State University, Manhattan. Konza Prairie is largely a portion of more extensive holdings developed by C. P. Dewey from 1872 to 1926 (Hulbert 1985).

With the acquisition of Konza Prairie and the advent in 1981 of the Long-Term Ecological Research (LTER) program, sponsored by the National Science Foundation (NSF), I and my students have been afforded the opportunity for both casual and systematic studies of prairie birds. This book is based on over twenty years of observations and provides a context for further explorations on the birds of the tallgrass prairie as well as a comparison with other biogeographic regions.

Although much of the fieldwork has been supported by the Long-Term Ecological Research program, additional support has been obtained from the NSF Undergraduate Research Program, the Chapman Fund of the American Museum of Natural History in New York City, the nongame wildlife program (Chickadee Check-off) of the Kansas Department of Wildlife and Parks, and the Bureau of General Research at Kansas State University. Indeed, without the assistance of these agencies considerably less would have been accomplished.

Konza Prairie is the dream of the late Professor Lloyd C. Hulbert, who through unstinting effort made it a reality. None of this would have happened without his dedication and devotion to the scientific importance of developing a tallgrass prairie research area. Lloyd's successors as director of Konza Prairie, Ted Barkley and Don Kaufman, as well as the various principal investigators of the LTER grant, Dick Marzolf, Don Kaufman, Tim Seastedt, and Alan Knapp, have continued in this heritage of dedication to prairie research. A great deal of thanks is due them all. Undergraduate research projects conducted over various periods by Bill Edelman, Jeff Fergen, Mark Fox, Martha Hall, Jennifer Harris, Scott Hatch, Jan Knodel, Rene Miller, Ken Petersen, Harvard Townsend, and Steve Wiegert have made important contributions to the understanding of prairie birds. Graduate research by Greg Farley, Elmer Finck, and Fred Mikesell on Konza Prairie provided more in-depth understanding of various aspects of the avian ecology of Konza Prairie. I am indebted to all of them for their excellent work.

Additionally I would like to thank Lou Ann Claassen for her secretarial assistance in the preparation of this manuscript and most of the figures, Jennifer DeLuca for preparation of additional figures, and Christy Knight for digitizing watershed and forest coverage maps. This book has been enhanced by the excellent photography of David Rintoul and James Holloway, for which I am very grateful. Thanks are due also to Professor Terry Johnson and members of the Division of Biology, who contributed to this effort in their various ways.

—*John L. Zimmerman*   xiii

Methods

The management plan and experimental design for Konza Prairie are based on watershed-sized areas undergoing burning that ranges in frequency from annually to every 20 years. These areas are grazed by cattle or bison or are ungrazed by any large herbivores (Fig. 1). Although short-term studies were conducted during the 1970s, systematic surveys of bird populations did not begin until 1981 with the establishment of permanent transect lines in unburned (20-year burn interval) watersheds, annually burned watersheds, watersheds burned every four years, and gallery and attenuated gallery forests. All the prairie watersheds with transects remained ungrazed by either cattle or bison during the period of this study. Beginning in 1992, however, some transects in each of the designated burning treatments are being grazed by bison.

The transects in unburned grasslands are located in 20B, 20C, 20D, and N20B; they total 3.27 km. During parts of the study period, transects in N4B, N4D, and N1B (total of 3.37 km) were also included in this data set, until initiation of the respective burning treatments in these watersheds. The transects in annually burned watersheds are in 1D and 1A and total 1.58 km. Transects in watersheds under the four-year burn interval are in 4A, 4B, and 4D; they have a total length of 1.62 km. All burning is completed during the first two weeks of April. The gallery forest transect is divided between the main stem and the north fork of Kings Creek and totals 1.62 km. The attenuated forest transect

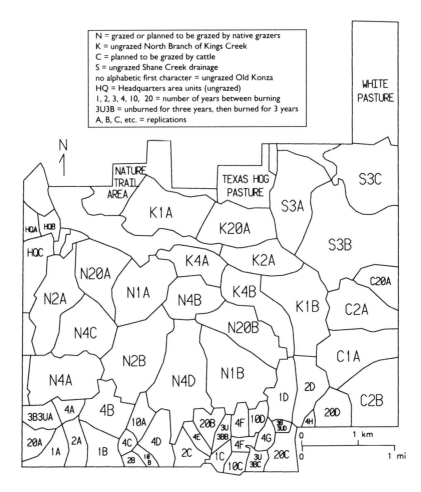

Figure 1. Experimental watersheds on Konza Prairie

is in upper Shane Creek for a total length of 1.30 km (see Frontispiece). Each transect is run twice a year: once during the first two weeks in January and again during the first two weeks of June. June data are presented for the years 1981 through 1990; January data are for 1982 through 1991.

Bird populations are estimated using the variable distance transect method of Burnham et al. (1980). This method can produce relative densities (individuals/ha) if sufficient records of

xvi

each type, about 40 observations, are obtained on a single transect. Using values less than this yields invalid density estimates. Since it has not been possible to obtain this number of records for all species in all watersheds, especially in winter, the data in this book are being reported as relative abundances (birds/km) to provide values for each species and permit comparisons between species, between habitats, and between seasons. This necessity, however, prevents direct comparisons to other habitats and locations for which density values are available. These transect data can provide relative densities if species values are combined—for example, by habitat. Furthermore, since it is the intent of LTER to demonstrate effects of long-term phenomena (i.e., climatic changes), we continue to collect these data by this method so that 50- to 100-year patterns can be quantified by combining years.

The transects to be run on a given day were selected at random, and no transect was started later than three hours after dawn. Furthermore, transects were not conducted if temperatures were below −26° Celsius (C), wind speeds were over 16 km per hour, or there was moderately heavy rain or snow. The observer proceeded along the transect line at a moderate pace (about 0.4 km/hour), stopping every 20 m or so to observe birds ahead and to either side of the transect. All birds seen within the watershed (or, in the case of forests, within the habitat) were counted and recorded by species. Birds flying overhead were not counted, with the exception of nighthawks and upland sandpipers involved in aerial territorial displays, which were counted. Swallows, raptors, and greater prairie-chickens were noted, but the quantitative data for these species are unreliable.

During late April and early May transects were covered by vehicle to locate prairie-chicken leks and count the number of males. One transect generally followed the divide between the north fork of Kings Creek and the watersheds of Shane Creek and Deep Creek. The other transect ran along the divide between the south fork of Kings Creek and Pressee Branch and   xvii

Swede Creek (see Frontispiece). Each transect was run twice, once in one direction and once in the other direction. The male population for a particular lek was the maximum number of males counted on one or more of these surveys.

The transect data and prairie-chicken counts comprise LTER data sets CBP01 and CPC01, respectively. Additionally, the bird species presence gathered from weekly or more frequent surveys is recorded by date (data set CBD01) and weekly over five-year intervals (data set CBC01). Furthermore, data related to all nesting observations are recorded (data set CBN01). All LTER data sets are available from the LTER Data Manager, Division of Biology at Kansas State University.

1 More Than Just Grass

Forecast by the remnant "oak openings" east of the Mississippi River, the beginning of the end of the eastern deciduous forest is definitely apparent where the broad-leaved forests that dominate the Ozark Plateau and hills bordering the Missouri River surrender to the increasingly effective rain shadow of the Rocky Mountains to form the forest-prairie mosaic of the Osage Plains and the glacial till north of the Kansas River. Although forest persists along rivers flowing down from the west and in well-watered valleys and draws that dissect the ancient uplands of the Flint Hills of Kansas, grasslands hold the higher ground. There the tallgrasses cling to shallower soils. Having adapted to withstand periodic fires that have swept across the landscape ever since the end of the last glacial episode, the tallgrasses are equipped with root systems that can extract the maximal amount of moisture available in the face of water stress imposed by the realities of limited rainfall and obligatory evapotranspiration.

The tallgrass prairie is not a unique flora (Wells 1970). There are very few endemic species, and none of them are grasses. A similar vegetation occurs in open habitats on the eastern coastal plain and in glades that interrupted the continuity of the deciduous forest that once dominated the landscape east of the Wabash River. During the Miocene-Pliocene transition, when the uplift of the western mountains reduced both the frequency and quantity of precipitation in the Great Plains, the broad evaporative surfaces of tree leaves proved to be poorly adapted to the increased aridity. Furthermore, the flat to rolling terrain created by the erosive effects of water on unglaciated surfaces and the deposition of wind-borne loess offered a topography that facilitated the spread of fires that are thought to have swept specific sites perhaps as frequently as every three or four years or at least every ten (Reichman 1987). All of these changes provided conditions that facilitated the migration of a grassland flora northward and westward from ancestral centers in southeastern North America (Anderson 1990), and the uniformity of conditions and the recentness of this development have permitted little subsequent diversification of the flora.

The avian fauna presents a similar picture. No endemic grassland species occur regularly in the tallgrass prairie (Mengel 1970). Like the prairie flora, the birds of the tallgrass prairie are derived from grassland habitats in other geographic areas, and there has been little fragmentation of grassland habitats for periods long enough to evolve reproductively isolated prairie populations. The role of the grasslands in the evolutionary history of North American birds has been primarily one of providing an isolating barrier between eastern and western populations of forest-adapted species. In short, the biogeographic importance of the Great Plains grasslands depends not upon what these communities are, but what they are not.

The tallgrass prairie, however, is more than just grass; it is a landscape covered by a patchwork of ecological communities that can exist under the climatic conditions of the region and the modifications imposed by a mosaic in soil composition, the impact of large grazers, and the serendipity of fire. In the Flint Hills Upland of Kansas where the tallgrass prairie has continued to exist close to its primeval state, forests dominated by either bur oak (see Appendix 2 for plant scientific names) or hackberry form narrow ribbons along the lower stream valleys, then become attenuated higher in the watersheds as interrupted stands of chinquapin oak, American elm, and redbud. On limestone outcrops that separate the interbedded layers of shale, forming

the distinctive Flint Hills profile, perched water tables offer sufficient moisture to support the thickets of dogwood, elm, plum,
and aromatic sumac that outline these rocky benches. And in between, the grasses and their herbaceous and woody associates
provide a mantle of vegetation that literally binds it all together
in a rich fabric of interlocking roots and a harlequin coat of leaf
shapes, textures, and hues. On arid claypan soils, grasses more
characteristic of the shortgrass plains dominate, and prairie
cordgrass and cattails, expatriates from distant coastal marshes
and eastern wetlands, form swales along the upper reaches of
the watersheds. The Flint Hills of Kansas provide a diverse ecological landscape that offers both aesthetic pleasure and biological interest.

On the basis of bird distribution, I have compartmentalized
this diversity into four ecological communities on Konza Prairie:
gallery forest, attenuated gallery forest, rock outcrop shrubs,
and grassland, either burned or unburned. An additional category is that of species characteristic of buildings and agricultural
land (Table 1). The quantitative data available for all residents except raptors, greater prairie-chickens, and swallows and for all
communities except the group of birds associated with rock outcrop shrubs provide averages for species richness (Fig. 2) and
relative abundances (Fig. 3) in both winter and summer.

These associations of species are just that; they are groups of
species that are distributed in the same biogeographic area because
of their particular evolutionary and dispersal histories and that occur together in similar habitats because they have certain basic environmental requirements in common (see Bock 1987). Although in
this sense their responses are individualistic (Gleason 1939), the
species do not exist together because of mere coincidence. These
communities form a continuum of increasing structural complexity
from burned grassland, to unburned grassland, to rock outcrop
shrubs, to attenuated gallery forest, to gallery forest—all ordered by
differences in soil moisture and fire frequency (see Whittaker 1951).
Hence, these communities are not discrete. Although some species

3

TABLE 1 Distribution of Species by Community (excluding strictly aquatic habitats)

GALLERY FOREST

Summer residents	Northern cardinal
Green-backed heron	Rose-breasted grosbeak
Wood duck	Indigo bunting
Red-tailed hawk	Northern oriole
Northern bobwhite	Winter residents
Yellow-billed cuckoo	Red-tailed hawk
Eastern screech-owl	Eastern screech-owl
Great horned owl	Great horned owl
Barred owl	Barred owl
Chuck-will's-widow	Belted kingfisher
Ruby-throated hummingbird	Red-headed woodpecker
Belted kingfisher	Red-bellied woodpecker
Red-headed woodpecker	Downy woodpecker
Red-bellied woodpecker	Hairy woodpecker
Downy woodpecker	Northern flicker
Hairy woodpecker	Blue jay
Northern flicker	American crow
Eastern wood-pewee	Black-capped chickadee
Eastern phoebe	Tufted titmouse
Great-crested flycatcher	White-breasted nuthatch
Northern rough-winged	Brown creeper
swallow	Carolina wren
Blue jay	Winter wren
American crow	Golden-crowned kinglet
Black-capped chickadee	European starling
Tufted titmouse	Northern cardinal
White-breasted nuthatch	Rufous-sided towhee
Carolina wren	American tree sparrow
House wren	Song sparrow
Blue-gray gnatcatcher	Harris' sparrow
Eastern bluebird	Dark-eyed junco
American robin	American goldfinch
European starling	Summer visitors
Warbling vireo	Wild turkey
Red-eyed vireo	Yellow warbler
Northern parula	Black-and-white warbler
Louisiana waterthrush	Scarlet tanager
Kentucky warbler	Common grackle
Brown-headed cowbird	Migrants
Summer tanager	Sharp-shinned hawk

4

Cooper's hawk
Whip-poor-will
Yellow-bellied sapsucker
Olive-sided flycatcher
Least flycatcher
Red-breasted nuthatch
Ruby-crowned kinglet
Veery
Gray-cheeked thrush
Swainson's thrush
Hermit thrush
Wood thrush
Cedar waxwing
Solitary vireo
Tennessee warbler
Orange-crowned warbler
Nashville warbler
Chestnut-sided warbler
Magnolia warbler
Yellow-rumped warbler
Black-throated green warbler
Blackburnian warbler

Pine warbler
Blackpoll warbler
American redstart
Ovenbird
Mourning warbler
Wilson's warbler
Chipping sparrow
Clay-colored sparrow
Fox sparrow
Lincoln's sparrow
Swamp sparrow
White-throated sparrow
White-crowned sparrow
Rusty blackbird
Purple finch
Winter visitors
Northern goshawk
Long-eared owl
House finch
Pine siskin
Evening grosbeak

ATTENUATED GALLERY FOREST

Summer residents
Red-tailed hawk
American kestrel
Northern bobwhite
American woodcock
Mourning dove
Yellow-billed cuckoo
Eastern screech-owl
Great horned owl
Red-headed woodpecker
Red-bellied woodpecker
Downy woodpecker
Hairy woodpecker
Northern flicker
Eastern wood-pewee
Eastern phoebe
Great crested flycatcher
Eastern kingbird
Blue jay
American crow

Black-capped chickadee
White-breasted nuthatch
Bewick's wren
House wren
Blue-gray gnatcatcher
Eastern bluebird
American robin
Gray catbird
Brown thrasher
Loggerhead shrike
European starling
Warbling vireo
Northern cardinal
Blue grosbeak
Indigo bunting
Rufous-sided towhee
Field sparrow
Lark sparrow
Red-winged blackbird
Common grackle

Continued   5

Table 1, continued

Brown-headed cowbird
Orchard oriole
Northern oriole
Winter residents
  Red-tailed hawk
  American kestrel
  Northern bobwhite
  Eastern screech-owl
  Great horned owl
  Red-headed woodpecker
  Red-bellied woodpecker
  Downy woodpecker
  Hairy woodpecker
  Northern flicker
  Blue jay
  American crow
  Black-capped chickadee
  Tufted titmouse
  White-breasted nuthatch
  Eastern bluebird
  European starling
  Northern cardinal
  Rufous-sided towhee
  American tree sparrow
  Song sparrow
  Harris' sparrow
  Dark-eyed junco
  American goldfinch
Summer visitors
  Yellow warbler
  Black-and-white warbler

Migrants
  Mississippi kite
  Sharp-shinned hawk
  Cooper's hawk
  Yellow-bellied sapsucker
  Olive-sided flycatcher
  Willow flycatcher
  Least flycatcher
  Ruby-crowned kinglet
  Cedar waxwing
  Tennessee warbler
  Orange-crowned warbler
  Nashville warbler
  Chestnut-sided warbler
  Magnolia warbler
  Yellow-rumped warbler
  Black-throated green warbler
  American redstart
  Wilson's warbler
  Yellow-breasted chat
  Lazuli bunting
  Chipping sparrow
  Clay-colored sparrow
  Fox sparrow
  Lincoln sparrow
  Swamp sparrow
  White-throated sparrow
  White-crowned sparrow
  Rusty blackbird
  Purple finch
Winter visitors
  Pine siskin

ROCK OUTCROP SHRUBS AND SHRUBBY SEEPS

Summer residents
  Black-billed cuckoo
  Bewick's wren
  Gray catbird
  Northern mockingbird
  Brown thrasher
  Bell's vireo
  Northern cardinal
  Field sparrow
  Brown-headed cowbird
  American goldfinch

Winter residents
  Black-capped chickadee
  American tree sparrow
  Song sparrow
  American goldfinch
Summer visitors
  Yellow warbler
Migrants
  White-eyed vireo
Winter visitors
  Mountain bluebird

GRASSLAND

Summer residents
  Northern harrier
  Ring-necked pheasant
  Greater prairie-chicken
  Northern bobwhite
  Upland sandpiper
  Mourning dove
  Common nighthawk
  Common poor-will
  Eastern kingbird
  Horned lark
  Northern rough-winged
    swallow
  Sedge wren
  Loggerhead shrike
  Common yellowthroat
  Dickcissel
  Lark sparrow
  Grasshopper sparrow
  Henslow's sparrow
  Red-winged blackbird
  Eastern meadowlark
  Brown-headed cowbird
Winter residents
  Northern harrier
  Rough-legged hawk
  American tree sparrow
  Dark-eyed junco
Summer visitors
  Turkey vulture
  Swainson's hawk
  Barn owl

  Western kingbird
  Scissor-tailed flycatcher
  Purple martin
  Cliff swallow
  Barn swallow
  Western meadowlark
Migrants
  Merlin
  Peregrine falcon
  Prairie falcon
  Lesser golden-plover
  Marbled godwit
  Franklin's gull
  Ring-billed gull
  Burrowing owl
  Short-eared owl
  Rock wren
  American pipit
  Sprague's pipit
  Vesper sparrow
  Lark bunting
  Savannah sparrow
  Le Conte's sparrow
  Lapland longspur
  Smith's longspur
  Chestnut-collared longspur
  Bobolink
  Brewer's blackbird
Winter visitors
  Golden eagle
  Barn owl
  Snow bunting

AGRICULTURALLY DISTURBED/CULTURAL HABITATS

Killdeer
Rock dove

Chimney swift
House sparrow

Some species are listed as both summer and winter residents because there is no information from which to conclude that the population is permanently resident. Species classified as visitors either breed in other habitats or sites or are not sedentary in the habitat in winter.

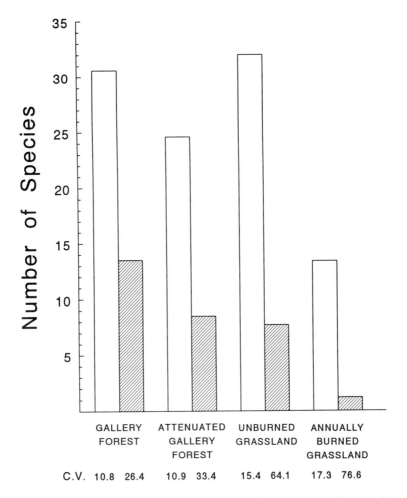

Figure 2. Means of species richness (N = 10) for June (open bars) and January (hatched bars) in major habitats (C.V. = coefficient of variation)

(for instance, the Henslow's sparrow and Bewick's wren) are restricted to a specific community or habitat type, most species occur across several communities in this continuum even though they are most frequent in only one of them. Since groups of species share the same pattern of relative frequencies (Figs. 4 through 8), it is convenient to categorize them into named communities.

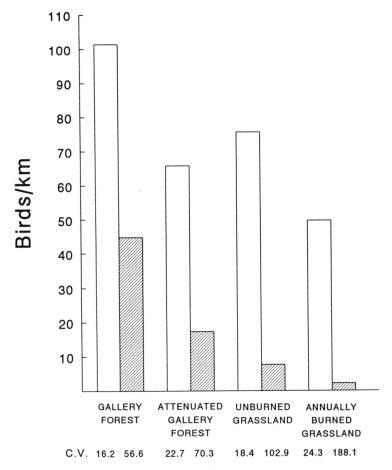

Figure 3. Means for relative abundances (birds/kilometer [km],
N = 10) for June (open bars) and January (hatched bars) in major habitats (C.V. = coefficient of variation)

Superimposed on this spatially heterogeneous landscape is
the variability among the birds in their temporal presence (Fig.
9). Of the 208 species known for Konza Prairie, only 27 species
(13 percent) occur as both summer and winter residents. Of
these, over two-thirds are found in the more structured forest
habitats, and less than a fifth (five species) inhabit the exposed

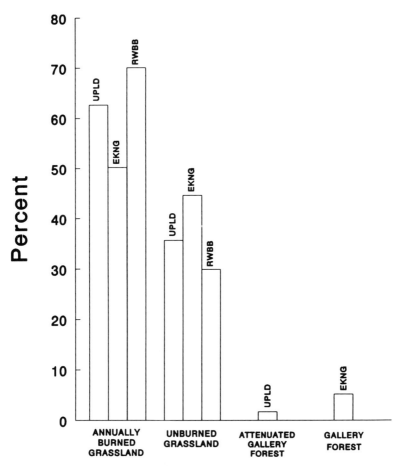

Figure 4. Breeding birds whose frequencies of relative abundances (percentage of total numbers) are greatest in annually burned grassland. For the upland sandpiper (UPLD) this reflects a feeding preference, since unburned grassland is the primary nesting habitat. The numbers of eastern kingbirds (EKNG) are similar in the two grassland habitats. Of the woody-dependent grassland birds, this is the only species not adversely affected by fire, since it prefers to nest in isolated trees that are usually untouched by most burns. That the highest numbers of red-winged blackbirds (RWBB) are in annually burned grassland results from the chance presence of good cattail stands in these watersheds.

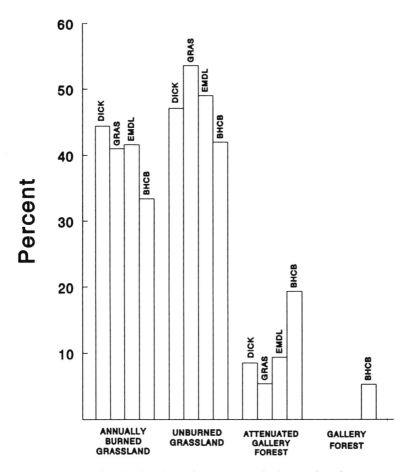

Figure 5. Breeding birds whose frequencies of relative abundances (percentage of total numbers) are greatest in unburned grassland. The dickcissel (DICK), grasshopper sparrow (GRAS), and eastern meadowlark (EMDL) are all grass-dependent species that occur every year during the breeding season in the grassland community, and their numbers are not significantly different in annually burned and unburned prairie. The brown-headed cowbird (BHCB) parasitizes hosts in all communities and thus is habitat independent, but a greater proportion of grassland species than forest species serve as its hosts. Other species that show this same pattern are loggerhead shrike, common yellowthroat, and Henslow's sparrow.

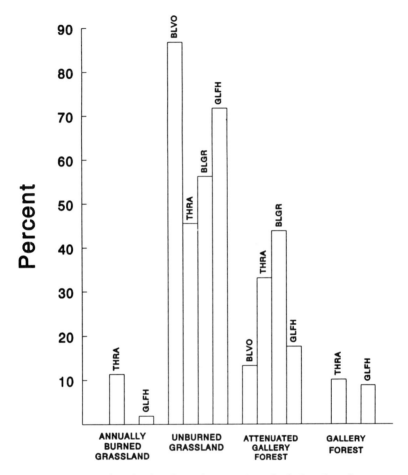

Figure 6. Breeding birds whose frequencies of relative abundances (percentage of total numbers) are greatest in unburned grassland because of their dependence upon woody vegetation, especially the development of the rock outcrop shrubs within these watersheds. The brown thrasher (THRA) and American goldfinch (GLFH) have a broader habitat spectrum than the more restricted Bell's vireo (BLVO) and blue grosbeak (BLGR). Other species that demonstrate this same pattern are gray catbird and rufous-sided towhee.

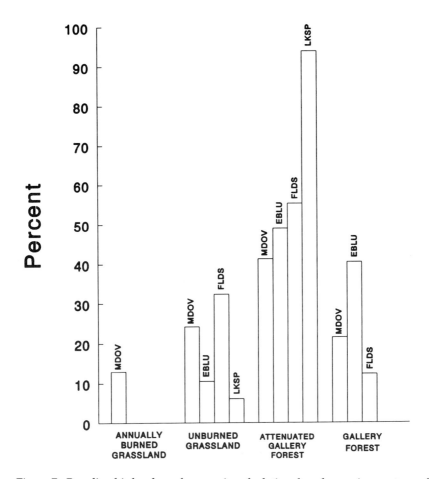

Figure 7. Breeding birds whose frequencies of relative abundances (percentage of total numbers) are greatest in the attenuated gallery forest. The mourning dove (MDOV) shows broad preference, but there is a seasonal pattern. In April and May the mourning dove is more abundant in the grassland community, where it nests on the ground, but by the time these data were collected in June, more individuals have begun nesting in forested habitats after the trees have leafed out. The habitat preference of the field sparrow (FLDS) is almost as broad, its only requirement being small shrubs in which to nest. The eastern bluebird (EBLU) is dependent on tree cavities and does find unused holes in isolated trees in unburned watersheds. Even though the lark sparrow (LKSP) nests on the ground, it prefers sparser ground cover than can be found in grassland communities, especially in annually burned watersheds where grass stem density is very high. Other species that show this same pattern are black-billed cuckoo and Bewick's wren.

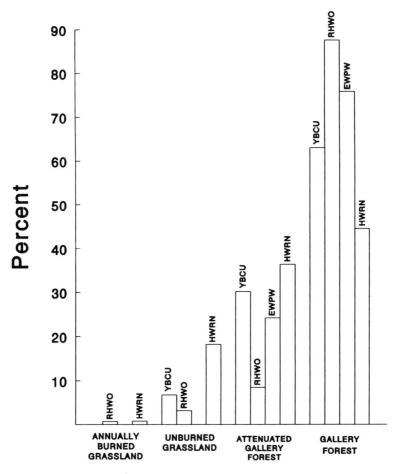

Figure 8. Breeding birds whose frequencies of relative abundances (percentage of total numbers) are greatest in the gallery forest. These are the true forest community species, although red-headed woodpeckers (RHWO) and house wrens (HWRN) will nest in isolated trees in grassland habitat. The yellow-billed cuckoo (YBCU) also nests in small trees that regularly occur in unburned grassland watersheds. The eastern wood-pewee (EWPW), however, is restricted to forested habitat, never selecting territories in isolated tree patches beyond the end of continuous forest. Many species illustrate this same pattern—all woodpeckers, eastern phoebe, great crested flycatcher, blue jay, black-capped chickadee, tufted titmouse, blue-gray gnatcatcher, red-eyed vireo, summer tanager, northern cardinal, and indigo bunting, to name a few.

Seasonal Status

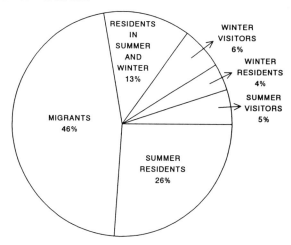

Habitat Distribution

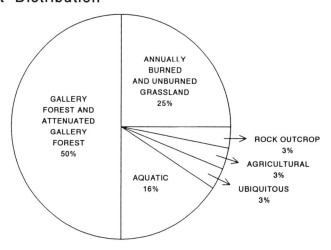

Figure 9. Frequency distribution of all species (N = 208) by seasonal status and habitat preference. Ubiquitous species showed no habitat preference. Agricultural habitat includes areas around buildings.

grasslands. Breeding season residents and visitors that invade the region to take advantage of the flush of food and the benign summer climate make up 31 percent of the species. Only 10 percent of the recorded species migrate from more northerly breeding grounds to remain throughout the winter. By far the most abundant seasonal pattern is that of the migrants; almost half of the species recorded for Konza Prairie occur only in the spring and fall during their periods of passage between breeding sites and contranuptial areas.

Konza Prairie offers a variety of avian surprises for the casual observer as well as the serious bird watcher (and the bird biologist) because of its midcontinental location and the ecological diversity of the landscape of this premier prairie research center. On sufficiently sized tracts of unburned prairie in which patches of standing dead grasses mottle the rolling sea of living forbs and grasses, the enigmatic Henslow's sparrow arrives to breed in late April, and then in late July sedge wrens appear from haunts unknown to build their nests in the ranker stands of grass along the upper reaches of prairie watersheds. (Did these same individuals breed elsewhere earlier in the summer?) In the evening during the breeding season, a driver along the main trail will see the ruby reflections of the eyes of poorwills before the birds flush at the very last moment from the gravel in front of the vehicle. On a May night, four species of nightjars can be heard (if the wind is still). Throughout the heat of summer the seemingly quiet, sterile bands of rough-leaved dogwood that outline the limestone ledges in both burned and unburned prairie erupt with pairs of scolding Bell's vireos. And in late August these shrubby borders are filled with hundreds of migrant eastern kingbirds devouring the fat-laden berries. They must recoup energy stores lost in yesterday's flight to prepare for the long journey to Amazonia. In the deep summer shade along the edge of the stream in the gallery forest a Louisiana waterthrush teeters in its quest for insects, and a summer tanager sings its hoarse song unseen in the canopy. If the bur oak crop has been ample, red-headed woodpeckers remain in large numbers within the gallery forest, filling the stillness of winter with their raucous chatter.

In this book you will find additional pictures and patterns, and I am sure you will discover even more of these. This discussion will serve as your introduction to the birds of the Konza Prairie Research Natural Area, and the various analyses will offer some insight into the ecological relationships among the species of birds inhabiting this last extensive fragment of the true prairie. I hope you will find that it is not a place "where the sedge is withered on the creek and no birds sing" (Rhodes 1991:153).

2   The Grassland Community

The sea of grass, a common metaphor in the literature of the prairie, conveys both reality and subjective impressions. Like the ocean, grassland is not a homogeneous habitat. Topography, climate, fire frequency, and grazing intensity—like salinity, currents, temperature, and depth in marine environments—affect species composition, the dominances of individual species, and in turn the physical structure of the community. Although we do not know all the ways the vegetation affects bird populations, we do know that plants are the component of the ecosystem that converts radiant energy of sunlight into chemical energy of organic compounds and thus provides the nutritional base for all animal populations. Birds use the seeds and fruits that plants produce or feed on the insects, reptiles, and mammals that gained their sustenance from plant bodies. It is less clear how the structure of the vegetative substrate affects birds. Some birds do prefer specific plants in which to build their nests. The physical openness of the habitat—that is, the heights and the density of the plants and the amounts of litter and standing dead vegetation—also is a component of the ecological niche of grassland species. Suffice it to say that an awareness of factors that affect vegetation provides the dynamic context in which we attempt to understand bird communities.

18   The grassland community of Konza Prairie is dominated by

big bluestem across all sites (Abrams and Hulbert 1987). This species and other warm-season grasses (little bluestem, Indian grass, and switchgrass) characterize the tallgrass prairie of the Kansas Flint Hills. Such mid-sized, warm-season grasses as sideoats grama and tall dropseed and cool-season grasses such as Kentucky bluegrass, Scribner panicum, Canada wild rye, and prairie junegrass, in combination with a delightful variety of annual and perennial forbs and several characteristic woody species (e.g., buckbrush, New Jersey tea, aromatic sumac, and rough-leaved dogwood), contribute to the diversity of the community. On the most xeric, upland sites shortgrasses like blue grama and hairy grama dominate small patches of the vegetation.

Although big bluestem's prevalence is not affected by topography, other species do vary between upland sites with shallow soil and lowland sites with deeper soil, producing variegated plant community patterns and differences in productivity. For example, both switchgrass and lead plant have significantly greater coverage on lowland sites (Abrams and Hulbert 1987) than on upland sites. Above-ground biomass production is greater on lowland soils, and seed production is usually greater as well, since there is a positive correlation between biomass production in the growing season and seed set in autumn (Briggs, Seastedt, and Gibson 1989). However, even though productivity is lower in the uplands, species richness is greater on these more elevated sites (Abrams and Hulbert 1987; Gibson 1989).

Fire is an integral aspect of the tallgrass prairie environment, and in its absence woody plants invade and eventually dominate the habitat, converting the prairie into a brushy woodland of cedar, elm, and dogwood. Indeed, "while a combination of selective forces, including climate, substrate, and grazers, was responsible for the evolution of grasses, fire has become the guardian of the tallgrass prairie" (Reichman 1987: 105). Prairie plants have obviously evolved under the influence of fire's ef- 19 fects. For example, the meristematic tissue of the warm-season grasses is protected from destruction by fires by means of the adaptation of being buried within plant tissue below the litter layer, and the translocation of organic compounds from the vulnerable above-ground foliage to fireproof underground storage in roots and rhizomes is accomplished as soon as possible after the end of the growing season.

The direct effect of fire is to cause a significant decrease in the coverage of woody vegetation by the elimination of entire plants or by the killing of their terminal meristems, reducing their coverage. Fire in the spring also decreases coverage by cool-season grasses like Kentucky bluegrass (Gibson 1989) and adversely affects forbs like heath aster (Hulbert 1986) and ironweed (Knapp 1984a); conversely, it stimulates others like Pitcher's sage (Abrams and Hulbert 1987). The net effect of fire is that the dominance of the warm-season grasses is increased at the expense of interstitial forbs and woody plants, which decreases species richness as well as the spatial heterogeneity of the plant community (Collins and Gibson 1990).

A major impact on the character of the prairie community is that fire removes standing dead vegetation and litter. This removal is critical, because the foliage of the warm-season grasses does not disintegrate and drop to the litter layer during annual senescence. Rather, it remains in place until fire, snow, or large grazers remove or compact this dead material. Compacted litter requires three to four years for complete decomposition (Kucera et al. 1967), this slow rate being a function of its poor nutrient quality (Koelling and Kucera 1965). If not removed, the litter can accumulate over the years to as much as 1,500 grams per square meter (g/m^2), equaling as much as two or three times the annual production (Weaver and Rowland 1952).

The standing dead stems and litter intercept the photosynthetically active portion of the solar spectrum, reducing this radiant energy to levels less than 1 percent of that measured above the canopy of the grass (Knapp 1984b) and hence retarding the

light-driven processes of energy and carbon fixation. In unburned prairie, measurements of leaf thickness, leaf mass, and
stomatal densities are all lower than in burned prairie, further reducing the ability of the plants to carry on photosynthesis
(Knapp 1985). The reduced amount of energy reaching the soil
surface also results in a lower soil temperature, which in spring
delays shoot emergence and reduces the amount of tillering
(sprouting from the base of a plant). Stem densities on unburned prairie are thus significantly decreased (Dokken and
Hulbert 1978). Warm-season grasses have an obligatory symbiotic relationship with mycorrhizal fungi in the soil, and in the
presence of litter, decreased soil warming in unburned prairie
decreases the activity of these organisms, contributing significantly to reduced vigor of prairie grasses (Bentivenga and Hetrick 1991).

Standing dead material and litter also intercept twice as
much of the rainfall as compared to the vegetation on prairie that
has been burned, resulting in a decrease in the amount of moisture reaching the soil surface (Gilliam, Seastedt, and Knapp
1987). Furthermore, the huge population of bacteria living on
the dead tissues in litter withdraws a significant amount of the
inorganic nitrogen available in precipitation, so that less of this
critical nutrient reaches the soil than in burned prairie (Seastedt
1985).

All these effects function to reduce primary production of
grasses in unburned tallgrass prairie (Knapp and Seastedt 1986),
so that the annual increase in above-ground biomass of the dominant big bluestem in sites burned early in the growing season
can be more than twice that of unburned sites (Hulbert 1988).
The reduced amount of active plant tissue in unburned prairie
reduces evaporative cooling, so that leaf temperatures of grass
can be as much as 9° Celsius (C) greater than that of adjacent
burned sites (Knapp 1984b), a condition that increases water
stress and still further adversely affects the productivity of these
grasses. Another effect of the impaired vitality of grasses in un-

21

burned prairie is to decrease the effectiveness of their roots in re-
moving the reduced amount of nitrogen that makes its way into
soil water, although the demands generated by low rates of production do not produce a severe nitrogen limitation on unburned prairie compared to that typical of more photosynthetically active burned prairie (Briggs, Seastedt, and Gibson 1989).
The net result of the reduction in evapotranspiration and the
lower nitrogen demand in unburned prairie is higher soil moisture and greater loss of water and nitrogen to surface drainage
and groundwater than from burned watersheds (McArthur et al.
1985).

The amount of standing dead vegetation and litter does, of
course, increase in the absence of fire, but only up to a point.
The accumulation of dead material reaches a relatively stable in-
crement after about four to six years, when the negative feedback effect of the reduction of productivity balances the rate of
decay (Abrams, Knapp, and Hulbert 1986). The increase and
subsequent stabilization of litter and standing dead vegetation
also inhibit germination and growth of many species, especially
annuals; an initial increase in species diversity in the first half
dozen or so years after a fire then begins to decrease (Collins and
Gibson 1990).

Certain watersheds on Konza Prairie are burned only every
four years. As should be expected from results on annually
burned prairie, there is a decrease in woody plant and forb coverage and elimination of litter and standing dead vegetation in
the year of the fire. Forb coverage and biomass of litter and
standing dead material then increase over the three years following the year of the fire (Gibson and Hulbert 1987; Gibson 1988).
Grass biomass, on the other hand, is highest after fire but then
decreases during the third and fourth postfire years, apparently
as a result of the negative feedback effect of increasing litter and
standing dead vegetation. There is no predictable pattern, however, in grasshopper populations as a function of time since fire
(Evans 1988a).

Drought affects plant production. J. Briggs and A. Knapp (personal communication) have shown that March soil moisture is the best predictor of subsequent above-ground biomass. During growing seasons when rainfall is deficient, the difference in productivity between burned and unburned prairie is obliterated (Briggs, Seastedt, and Gibson 1989). During the drought of 1988 and 1989, for example, unburned sites actually outproduced annually burned watersheds (J. Briggs, personal communication). It is worthwhile to note, however, that productivity on burned prairie during the growing season following a season of drought is especially great. This comeback appears to be the result of decreased productivity during the year of drought, which in turn results in less depletion of soil nitrogen so that in the following year the growth of grasses in the burned watersheds is less limited by nitrogen availability (Hayes 1985).

Since grazing by bison is a treatment applied to about a third of the area of the grassland community on Konza Prairie, including—in 1992—all transects in N-designated watersheds, it is important to appreciate the significant impact of grazing on characteristics of the prairie community. Bison preferentially graze big bluestem, selecting patches with lower forb species richness and cover and a higher grass-to-forb ratio (Vinton et al. in press). In the growing season, bison are three times more likely to be found on recently burned watersheds in which warm-season grass productivity is higher than on unburned sites. Bison do graze in unburned watersheds but similarly select patches dominated by big bluestem. Because of the greater spatial heterogeneity of unburned prairie, preferred patches are smaller and more widely spaced; this pattern leads to grazing effects that are more scattered and locally smaller than in burned prairie. Thus bison are likely to enhance the heterogeneity of unburned prairie even further (Vinton et al. in press).

Grazing augments the relative growth rates of both big bluestem and switchgrass compared to ungrazed controls (Vinton and Hartnett 1992). In big bluestem, however, this compensatory response has a negative effect on productivity in the subsequent growing season, perhaps through its costs to allocation of stored resources. Removal of grass biomass decreases amounts of standing dead matter and litter that are produced in a season and thus reduces the negative effect of this material on primary production in subsequent years, tending perhaps to counteract the negative physiological impacts of grazing on individual big bluestem tillers. Although the selective grazing by bison of grasses, especially big bluestem, enhances light availability to adjacent forbs by as much as 70 percent, the increase in total forb biomass that might be expected from the assumed reduction in competition for light is seldom detected except in upland sites (Fahnestock and Knapp 1991). This result reflects a species-specific response by forbs to removal of grass. Biomass of both western ragweed and heath aster was greater in grazed patches, but ironweed and indigobush showed no significant differences (Ward et al. 1991).

Several watersheds on Konza Prairie are grazed by cattle during the growing season, which also changes species composition of the community (Weaver 1954; Herbel and Anderson 1959; Collins and Gibson 1990). Under light to moderate grazing big bluestem, little bluestem, Indian grass, and switchgrass decrease in their coverage, whereas Kentucky bluegrass, sideoats grama, blue grama, hairy grama, tall dropseed, and Scribner panicum increase. If grazing becomes too intense, all naturally occurring species decrease, and the community is invaded by annual bromes, little barley, tall fescue, western ragweed, thistles, vervain, and gumweed. During 1992, comprehensive studies of the impacts of cattle grazing on the prairie community were initiated, and bird transects will be added to this treatment beginning in the breeding season of 1993.

THE BREEDING-BIRD COMMUNITY

Grasslands of the world offer the least avian species diversity of any biome (Cody 1966). A set of species that includes some sort of grouselike bird, a seemingly out-of-place wader or two, a ground-nesting raptor, and a triad of small, medium, and large insectivores characterizes the community. Tallgrass prairie is no exception (Risser et al. 1981): On Konza Prairie the greater prairie-chicken, upland sandpiper, northern harrier, grasshopper sparrow, dickcissel, and eastern meadowlark along with the brown-headed cowbird (whose presence depends upon the "hospitality" of the three insectivores) are the characteristic breeding species.

The variety of birds in grassland and associated rock outcrop habitats at Konza Prairie (see Table 1) reflects the area's proximity to the eastern deciduous forest, since many species that occur are not grassland species but have invaded prairies from forested regions to the east (Mengel 1970) and are associated with woody vegetation. If just those species that are solely dependent on grass—what Martin Cody would call the "appropriate" species, and which I refer to as the grass-dependent core species (Fig. 10)—are enumerated, only nine species are present on unburned prairie during summer and no more than six on annually burned prairie. Although reliable quantitative data were not obtainable in this study, greater prairie-chicken, northern harrier, and the sedge wren (which does not arrive until July) should be added to this list.

Considering total relative abundance of all species in unburned prairie, four species (dickcissel, brown-headed cowbird, grasshopper sparrow, eastern meadowlark) make up over 50 percent of all individuals; in burned prairie these same most abundant species make up almost two-thirds of the total population. These species, along with the upland sandpiper, are typically the most abundant summer birds in tallgrass prairies of North America (Wiens 1973; Wiens and Dyer 1975). From a study of the ecological niches of these species, Rotenberry and Wiens (1980) demonstrated considerable breadth and overlap and little evidence for resource partitioning.

Although there is a constancy in the number of breeding-

25

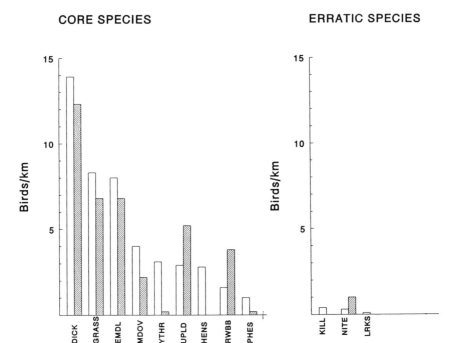

CORE SPECIES   ERRATIC SPECIES

Figure 10. Mean relative abundances (birds/km, N = 10) of grass-dependent species, 1981–1990, on June transects in unburned (open bars) and annually burned (hatched bars) grasslands, except for raptors, prairie-chickens, swallows, and species recorded in fewer than 20 percent of the years. Core species occurred every year on unburned grassland, but in annually burned grassland only DICK, EMDL, GRASS, MDOV, RWBB, and UPLD occurred every year. Erratic species occurred from 20 to 90 percent of the years. Grass-dependent species require grass/forb nesting substrate. DICK = dickcissel, EMDL = eastern meadowlark, GRASS = grasshopper sparrow, HENS = Henslow's sparrow, KILL = killdeer, LRKS = lark sparrow, MDOV = mourning dove, NITE = common nighthawk, PHES = ring-necked pheasant, RWBB = red-winged blackbird, UPLD = upland sandpiper, YTHR = common yellowthroat

season species from year to year in tallgrass prairie, their abundances vary. Wiens and Dyer (1975) surveyed a range of tallgrass habitats in North America, and the coefficient of variation (C.V.) for density averaged 37.2. As should be expected when only one site is considered, the coefficient of variation for relative abundances at Konza Prairie on June transects over the 10 years of this survey is lower: 18.4 in unburned prairie and 24.3 in burned prairie (Table 2). This difference in variance related to fire treatment reflects the greater degree of perturbation that arises from annual burning and the effect of periodic drought on bird abundances in burned prairie (see below).

Population trends from 1980 through 1989 for species recorded on the U.S. Fish and Wildlife Service's June breeding-bird survey have been calculated for Kansas (S. Droege, unpublished). These data can be compared to the populations of the same species in unburned grassland on Konza Prairie during the period 1981 through 1990 (Table 3). Using a sign test on runs (Dixon and Massey 1957:287–288), the numbers of northern bobwhite, Bell's vireo, common yellowthroat, rufous-sided towhee, and field sparrow show a significant increase during this period on Konza Prairie, whereas all the rest show no significant trends. Of 30 species shared between Konza Prairie and the Kansas analysis, there is agreement in trends (or lack of a significant trend) for 16 (53 percent). Of particular interest, however, are the significant declines in Kansas of mourning dove, eastern kingbird, red-winged blackbird, eastern meadowlark, dickcissel, and grasshopper sparrow, all of which are grassland core species (Figs. 10 and 11) that show no significant trends on Konza Prairie. The decline in these characteristic grassland birds in the state compared to their stability on Konza Prairie suggests a deterioration in the native pastures under the impact of agronomic practices. The significant increase in common yellowthroats on Konza, but not in Kansas, also supports this speculation.

All grass-dependent core species except the pheasant are resident only during summer. With the exception of brown-headed cowbird (Elliott 1980) and upland sandpiper (Bowen 1976), all breeding species are territorial. Most territorial birds are philopatric (eastern meadowlark, Lanyon 1957; grasshopper sparrow, Smith 1963; dickcissel, Zimmerman and Finck 1989), but some are not (Henslow's sparrow, J. L. Zimmerman, unpublished). Typically, philopatric birds are more patch dependent

27

TABLE 2 Annual Species Richness and Relative Abundance on June Transects in Annually Burned and Unburned Grassland

Year	All Species[a] Number	All Species[a] Birds/Km	Grass-Dependent Core Species[b] Number	Grass-Dependent Core Species[b] Birds/Km	Woody-Dependent Core Species and Erratic Species[c] Number	Woody-Dependent Core Species and Erratic Species[c] Birds/Km
			Unburned Grassland			
1981	26	52.4	9	34.1	16	11.0
1982	32	57.3	9	36.2	22	14.1
1983	35	69.2	9	44.1	25	18.5
1984	31	84.1	9	50.0	21	24.8
1985	34	76.8	9	47.2	24	21.0
1986	32	89.2	9	56.5	22	23.3
1987	33	98.5	9	54.0	23	33.5
1988	26	82.0	9	46.4	16	25.0
1989	23	71.6	9	45.9	13	19.9
1990	26	75.6	9	41.6	16	25.7
mean	29.8[d]	75.7[e]	9[f]	45.6[g]	19.8[h]	21.7[i]
S.E.	1.32	4.41	0	2.24	1.32	2.01
C.V.	14.0	18.4	0	15.5	21.0	29.3
			Annually Burned Grassland			
1981	12	48.7	6	38.6	5	5.7
1982	10	33.4	6	27.2	3	2.5
1983	10	44.3	7	32.3	2	1.9
1984	11	44.3	6	34.2	4	5.7
1985	11	41.8	6	34.8	4	3.2
1986	12	46.8	6	38.6	5	6.3
1987	14	74.7	8	55.1	5	7.0
1988	13	58.2	7	37.3	5	8.9
1989	15	41.8	7	27.8	7	9.5
1990	13	62.0	6	50.6	6	8.2
mean	12.1[d]	49.6[e]	6.5[f]	37.6[g]	4.6[h]	5.9[i]
S.E.	0.53	3.81	0.22	2.84	0.40	0.75
C.V.	13.8	24.3	10.9	23.8	31.1	45.0

[a]This category includes brown-headed cowbird and hence is greater than the sum of the other two categories. It excludes raptors, prairie-chickens, and swallows.

[b]Grass-dependent core species are dependent upon grass and/or forbs for nest sites and were present every year.

cWoody-dependent core species require woody plants for nest sites and occurred every year. Erratic species were recorded during 20 to 90 percent of the years and include both woody- and grass-dependent species.

dThe means for unburned and burned grassland are significantly different (Student's t = 12.5, df = 18, P < 0.01).

eThe means for unburned and burned grassland are significantly different (Student's t = 4.46, df = 18, P < 0.01).

fThe means for unburned and burned grassland are significantly different (Student's t = 11.4, df = 18, P < 0.01).

gExcluding values for Henslow's sparrow and common yellowthroat reduces mean in unburned grassland to 39.7 birds/km which is not significantly different from the mean for burned grassland.

hThese means are significantly different (Student's t = 10.86, df = 18, P < 0.01).

iThese means are significantly different (Student's t = 7.18, df = 18, P < 0.01).

and have narrower niche breadths (Wiens 1976; Rotenberry and Wiens 1980), but lack of philopatry in the tallgrass prairie may be related to the temporal unpredictability of fire. Site tenacity in Henslow's sparrow, for example, would be of little value if standing dead vegetation—a critical factor in its habitat requirements (Zimmerman 1988)—in last year's territory had been removed by fire. Although I disagree with Cody's (1985) contention that grassland birds are not typically philopatric, the Henslow's sparrow is one example that supports his notion of an absence of philopatry allowing species to track resource "hot spots." Mating patterns of these birds are various—monogamy (e.g., grasshopper sparrow, Smith 1968; Henslow's sparrow, Wiens 1969), polygyny (eastern meadowlark, Lanyon 1957; red-winged blackbird, Orians 1961; dickcissel, Zimmerman 1966), and promiscuity (brown-headed cowbird, Elliott 1980).

Only 29 percent of all species present in unburned prairie are present both winter and summer, and just 13 percent of the species are considered permanent residents in burned prairie (Table 4). This pattern of seasonal occurrence is similar to that observed in grazed prairies in Oklahoma (Grzybowski 1982). Even among permanent resident species, many—for instance, the greater prairie-chicken—move off the prairie to winter in adjacent agricultural habitats. The geographic patterns of the contranuptial area for summer residents in both unburned

29

TABLE 3 Abundance Trends in Unburned Grassland Species on June
Transects on Konza Prairie (1981–1990) Compared to Kansas Patterns
(1980–1989)[a]

	Konza Prairie	Kansas
Ring-necked pheasant	ns	ns
Northern bobwhite	increase	ns
Upland sandpiper	ns	ns
Mourning dove	ns	decrease
Yellow-billed cuckoo	ns	decrease
Common nighthawk	ns	ns
Red-headed woodpecker	ns	decrease
Northern flicker	ns	decrease
Great crested flycatcher	ns	ns
Eastern kingbird	ns	decrease
Blue jay	ns	ns
Black-capped chickadee	ns	ns
House wren	ns	ns
Eastern bluebird	ns	increase
American robin	ns	ns
Gray catbird	ns	decrease
Brown thrasher	ns	ns
European starling	ns	ns
Bell's vireo	increase	increase
Common yellowthroat	increase	ns
Northern cardinal	ns	ns
Dickcissel	ns	decrease
Rufous-sided towhee	increase	increase
Field sparrow	increase	ns
Grasshopper sparrow	ns	decrease
Red-winged blackbird	ns	decrease
Eastern meadowlark	ns	decrease
Brown-headed cowbird	ns	ns
Northern oriole	ns	ns
American goldfinch	ns	ns

ns = no significant trend

[a]Excluded are raptors, prairie-chickens, swallows, and species that occurred in
fewer than 50 percent of the years on June transects.

TABLE 4 Annual Species Richness and Seasonal Status on June Transects for All Grassland Species[a]

Year	Number	Resident Both Summer and Winter	Summer Resident Only	Winter Range of Summer Residents	
				North Temperate Zone	Neotropics
Unburned Grassland					
1981	28	9	19	12	7
1982	35	14	21	13	8
1983	40	13	27	17	10
1984	34	10	24	16	8
1985	35	10	25	15	10
1986	33	9	24	16	8
1987	36	11	25	14	11
1988	27	5	22	13	9
1989	25	5	20	14	6
1990	27	7	20	14	6
mean	32.0	9.3	22.7	14.4	8.3
S.E.	1.56	0.96	0.84	0.50	0.54
C.V.	15.4	32.5	11.8	11.0	20.5
%		29	71	63	37
Annually Burned Grassland					
1981	12	0	12	7	5
1982	12	2	10	6	4
1983	11	2	9	6	3
1984	12	2	10	6	4
1985	12	0	12	7	5
1986	14	2	12	8	4
1987	15	2	13	9	4
1988	14	2	12	6	6
1989	19	3	16	10	6
1990	13	2	11	8	3
mean	13.4	1.7	11.7	7.3	4.4
S.E.	0.73	0.30	0.62	0.45	0.34
C.V.	17.3	55.8	16.6	19.4	24.4
%		13	87	62	38

[a]Excluded are species that have occurred in fewer than 20 percent of the years on June transects.

31

and burned prairie are similar: Almost two-thirds winter within the north temperate zone, and the remainder spend the non-breeding season in the neotropics or south temperate zone (Table 4).

Although grazing by bison has been inaugurated on several watersheds in the last few years, quantitative data to assess this treatment as a factor in the organization of avian communities at Konza Prairie are not available. Kantrud's (1981) important study, which included tallgrass prairie regions of North Dakota, provided some indication of what might be expected when bison are moved into watersheds with bird transects. Species richness is inversely related to grazing intensity, but relative density increases proportionately to grazing intensity. This latter effect results from increased attractiveness of heavily grazed grasslands for species like upland sandpipers, killdeers, and horned larks. This is understandable because they forage in habitat of lowest vegetative cover; such an increase might be expected for Konza Prairie, except that grazing treatments might never reach an intensity high enough to produce such an effect. Population densities of common yellowthroats, sedge wrens, red-winged blackbirds, and grasshopper sparrows could be expected to be depressed in watersheds that would be mostly heavily grazed. Populations of western meadowlarks showed no response to grazing intensity (Kantrud 1981). As that result was paralleled by Dale (1984) but not by Wiens (1973), it is difficult to predict the response for eastern meadowlarks. Dickcissels were poorly represented in Kantrud's study, but lark buntings, the ecological counterpart of dickcissels in mixed and shortgrass prairie regions, were most abundant in moderately grazed sites. A caveat underlying these predictions is that grazing, by its very nature, is not a uniform treatment and that there is considerable geographic variation in reported responses (Wiens and Dyer 1975). Bison grazing on Konza Prairie has tended to make the vegetative community in burned watersheds even more homogeneous and that in unburned watersheds even more heterogeneous.

This suggests that any differences in the bird community that are based on the difference in burning treatment will be accentuated.

In the absence of significant grazing effects on most of Konza Prairie during the ten years of intensive data collection, fire is the principal factor affecting contemporary characteristics of the grassland bird community. Both the significant difference in species richness for all grassland species and the difference in relative abundance between burned and unburned grassland (Table 2) are the direct effect of fire on the vegetative structure of the habitat. Fire substantially reduces the presence of a whole suite of woody-dependent species that are perennially present on unburned prairie but are either absent or significantly less frequently found on burned prairie (Fig. 11). But even for grass-dependent species, fire reduces richness even further by elimination of the standing dead vegetation and litter that is critical for Henslow's sparrows (Zimmerman 1988) and probably for common yellowthroats as well. Thus in burned prairie, only six species occur every year (Fig. 10).

An early explanation for the paucity of the grassland avifauna was related to the simplicity of the habitat and suggested that grasslands provided an insufficient number of perches for territorial display (Kendeigh 1941). This hypothesis was experimentally investigated by Jan Knodel on Konza Prairie and not supported (Knodel-Montz 1981). An alternate hypothesis, similarly related to the simple habitat structure provided by grasslands, is that resources are limiting in grasslands and that the characteristic low species richness is a reflection of habitat saturation (Cody 1968). According to this hypothesis, there are not enough potential ways of making an ecological living in the simplistically structured and relatively reduced net productivity typical of grasslands, and competitive exclusion operates to keep species richness low.

In average and wet precipitation years, above-ground primary productivity in spring-burned grasslands is enhanced

33

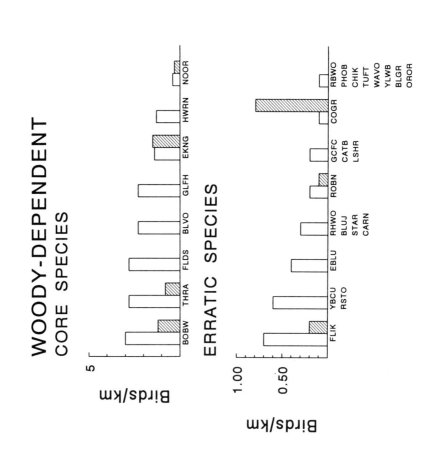

HABITAT-INDEPENDENT SPECIES

Birds/km

10

5

BHCB

Figure 11. Mean relative abundances (birds/km, N = 10) of woody-dependent and habitat-independent species, 1981–1990, on June transects in unburned (open bars) and annually burned (hatched bars) grasslands, except for raptors, prairie-chickens, swallows, and species recorded in fewer than 20 percent of the years. Core species occurred every year on unburned grassland. Erratic species occurred from 20 to 90 percent of the years. Woody-dependent species use shrubs and trees for nesting substrate, whereas the brown-headed cowbird (BHCB) is habitat independent since it parasitizes both grass-dependent and woody-dependent species. BLGR = blue grosbeak, BLUJ = blue jay, BLVO = Bell's vireo, BOBW = northern bobwhite, CARN = northern cardinal, CATB = gray catbird, CHIK = black-capped chickadee, COGR = common grackle, EBLU = eastern bluebird, EKNG = eastern kingbird, FLDS = field sparrow, FLIK = northern flicker, GCFC = great crested flycatcher, GLFH = American goldfinch, HWRN = house wren, LSHR = loggerhead shrike, NOOR = northern oriole, OROR = orchard oriole, PHOB = eastern phoebe, RBWO = red-bellied woodpecker, RHWO = red-headed woodpecker, ROBN = American robin, RSTO = rufous-sided towhee, STAR = European starling, THRA = brown thrasher, TUFT = tufted titmouse, WAVO = warbling vireo, YBCU = yellow-billed cuckoo, YLWB = yellow warbler

(Knapp and Seastedt 1986), which in turn increases the standing crop biomass of herbivorous insects (Evans 1988b). If the saturation hypothesis is valid, this augmentation in the resource base for the bird population should be reflected in an increase in relative abundance of birds on burned prairie. But the opposite happens (Table 2). There is a significant decrease in the woody-dependent core species and all erratically present species, but if the numbers are corrected for the absence of Henslow's sparrows and yellowthroats, there is no significant difference in relative abundances of the grass-dependent core species in unburned and burned grasslands (Fig. 12). The "appropriate" species do not increase, contrary to the expectation of this hypothesis.

It thus appears that birds in unburned prairie are not food-resource limited, since an increase in resources as a result of fire does not result in a significant increase in their populations. Trophic resources for prairie birds are at least adequate, perhaps even superabundant! This reality is reflected in Finck's (1984b) study of habitat selection in dickcissels. Even though oldfield habitats were preferred over prairie, this response was not related to food availability. If food were more limiting in prairie habitats than in oldfields, one could predict that more effort would have to be expended toward finding food in the prairie. But there was no difference in the time males spent foraging; in both habitats this activity required only about a third of their daily activity budgets. Energetic resources are more than adequate for the population of species occurring in prairies. The populations are maintained free of competitive restraint, their levels being regulated by other factors—for example, cowbird parasitism (Zimmerman 1988). If an energy surplus does indeed exist, no additional species have taken advantage of this potential. This may simply reflect the brevity of grasslands in evolutionary time.

Another alternate hypothesis for low grassland bird diversity was proposed by Wiens (1974), who suggested that periodic occurrence of drought functions as a bottleneck that permits

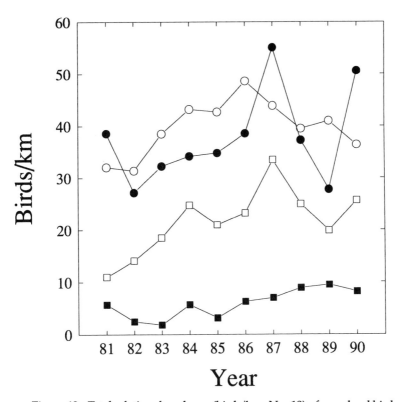

Figure 12. Total relative abundance (birds/km, N = 10) of grassland birds on June transects in annually burned and unburned grasslands, 1981–1990. Data for grass-dependent core species exclude values for Henslow's sparrows and common yellowthroats, since these species either do not occur or are minimally present on annually burned grasslands. Circles are grass-dependent core species in unburned grassland (open circles) and in annually burned grassland (solid circles). Squares denote woody-dependent core and erratic species in unburned (open squares) and annually burned (solid squares) grasslands.

only drought-adapted species to be perennially present in grass-land habitats. The low species richness reflects the reality that few species have evolved this ability in the grasslands of the world. If Wiens's hypothesis is valid, grassland birds should be able to maintain their population levels through periods of drought. The lack of correlation between abundances of grass-dependent core species on unburned prairie and March soil moisture supports this hypothesis (Zimmerman 1992); for these species, variations in moisture are irrelevant to their abundances. The relative abundances of woody-dependent species, on the other hand, do illustrate a positive correlation with soil moisture, a response to be expected for species in which drought has not been a prominent selective factor in their past evolution (Smith 1982). But when drought is coincident with fire, grass-dependent bird populations also are depressed. Then the reduction in plant productivity on burned prairie resulting from drought (Briggs, Seastedt, and Gibson 1989) brings the bird community to saturation, resulting in a decrease in relative abundance correlated with a decrease in moisture (Zimmerman 1992). But even though the numbers of species are diminished, species richness remains unchanged.

On watersheds burned every four years, abundances of grass-dependent core species of birds decrease the year of the fire but not significantly (Fig. 13). Furthermore, this value (37.2 ± 4.63 birds/km) is essentially identical to that measured on annually burned grasslands (37.6 ± 2.84 birds/km). Abundances of these species then increase, but not significantly, and during the next three years remain relatively stable at levels that are not significantly different from the abundance of these species on unburned grassland (45.6 ± 2.24 birds/km), even though the coverage by grass is decreasing. This lack of difference in the abundances of these species as a function of time since fire is paralleled by a similar response in annually burned and unburned grasslands (Table 2).

Relative abundances of woody-dependent species in watersheds burned every four years respond quite differently from what might be expected from abundances of these species in annually burned and unburned grasslands (Table 2). In the year of the fire, the number of woody-dependent and erratic species (16.9 ± 6.35 birds/km) is higher and significantly different from the population in annually burned grassland (5.9 ± 0.75 birds/

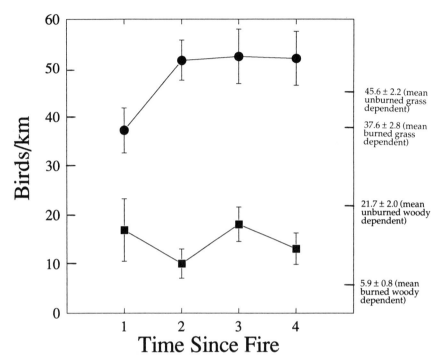

Figure 13. Mean relative abundances (birds/km ± S.E.) of grass-dependent core species (circles) and woody-dependent core and erratic species (squares) on June transects and time in years since fire (year 1 is the year of the fire). In order to make a valid comparison, values for Henslow's sparrows are excluded from the means for grass-dependent core species, since this species is not present in grasslands the year of the fire. These data for the year of the burn (year 1) are also corrected for a significant dependence upon March soil moisture by the function $y = -31.41 + 0.99x$, where x is the percent of maximum soil moisture transformed by an arcsine function. All data for the woody-dependent species have also been similarly corrected for their dependence on March soil moisture by the function $y = -5.32 + 0.42x$, where x is the percent of maximum soil moisture transformed by an arcsine function.

km) (Student's $t = 2.45$, df = 13, $P < 0.05$). Although none of the means for the three years following fire are significantly different from the value for the first year, there is a significant difference for the mean for year 2 (10.1 ± 2.95 birds/km) from the mean for these species on unburned prairie (21.7 ± 2.01 birds/km) (Student's t = 3.15, df = 13, P < 0.01) as well as a difference between the mean on unburned prairie and that measured in year 4 (13.1 ± 3.19 birds/km)(Student's t = 2.36, df = 13, P < 0.05). The mean for the third year is not different from that of unburned prairie.

Hence, burning, whether annually or every four years, has no significant effect on the populations of grass-dependent core species (with the exception of Henslow's sparrows and common yellowthroats during the year of the burn). For the woody-dependent species, however, the impact of burning every year as opposed to every four years is greater because of the more effective suppression of woody vegetation by annual burning. Similarly, the woody-dependent bird species maintain generally significantly higher populations on unburned prairie than can be obtained in grasslands that are affected by fire on a four-year interval.

The role of birds in the grassland ecosystem has been succinctly summarized by Wiens (1973:265): "It seems unlikely that birds exert any major influence on ecosystem structure, functional properties, or dynamics through their general effects on either the flux rate or storage of energy or nutrients." The highest energy demand for the entire breeding-season bird population calculated for a tallgrass prairie site (Osage prairie) by Wiens and Dyer (1975) was a value of 2.9 kilocalories (kcal)/m². Almost 50 percent of the food consumed by the birds at this location was chewing, herbivorous insects (primarily grasshoppers). Following the calculations of Schartz and Zimmerman (1971), the consumption of only eight to nine grasshoppers for each square meter of prairie would satisfy the total energy demand of the bird community across the complete span of the breeding season! Given the ease at which such an energy income could be obtained, it is not surprising that competition for energetic resources does not drive the structuring of the grassland breeding-bird community. This is not to say that grassland birds do not affect herbivorous insect populations. They do reduce both densities and species richness (Joern 1986). But normally, in my opinion, the food resource is more than ample. Determining at what prey level food would become limiting would be valuable. Perhaps this level is reached in burned grassland during seasons of drought. Although the energy demand on other habitats—for example, northern coniferous forest—may be ten times as great as that of prairie (Wiens 1975), the participation by birds in any ecosystem's energy flow during the breeding season is, in general, slight. Winter, however, may present more stringent conditions for obtaining adequate energy resources (Fretwell 1972).

WINTER BIRD POPULATIONS

During the ten years of transect data collection, 21 species have been recorded at least 20 percent of the time in unburned prairie on January transects. The mean species richness is only 7.7 (Fig. 2). On annually burned prairie it is even less, averaging only 1.2 species. Not only are there even fewer species in tallgrass prairie during winter, there are fewer individuals (Fig. 14). Indeed, in some winters no birds are recorded on January transects in burned watersheds.

The only consistent species is the American tree sparrow, which has been recorded every year in unburned grassland and 50 percent of the years in burned prairie. Its numbers, however, are low (averaging 2.21 ± 1.32 birds/km on burned watersheds and 5.47 ± 2.28 birds/km on unburned watersheds) and highly variable (coefficients of variation equal to 188 and 132, respectively). Since burned prairie has greater primary productivity during an average rainfall year (Briggs, Seastedt, and Gibson 1989) and hence greater seed set (Knapp and Hulbert 1986), I expected relative abundances of these sparrows would be greater during winter on annually burned prairie. But the reverse appears to be the case; there are more birds on unburned watersheds, except that these means are not significantly different (Student's $t = 1.24$, $P > 0.05$). At a similar latitude in the Great

41

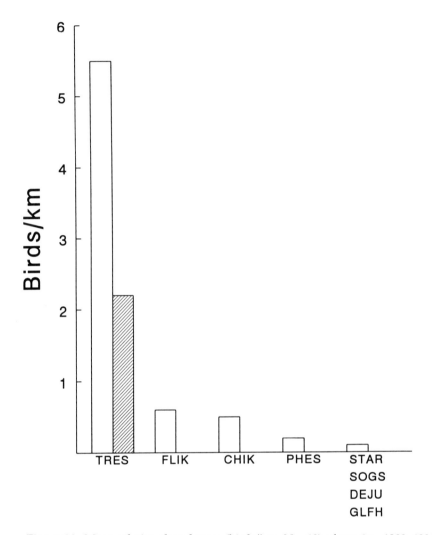

Figure 14. Mean relative abundances (birds/km, N = 10) of species, 1982–1991, on January transects in unburned (open bars) and annually burned (hatched bars) grasslands, except for raptors, prairie-chickens, and species occurring in fewer than 20 percent of the years. CHIK = black-capped chickadee, DEJU = dark-eyed junco, FLIK = northern flicker, GLFH = American goldfinch, PHES = ring-necked pheasant, SOGS = song sparrow, STAR = European starling, TRES = American tree sparrow. The following species had means < 0.10 birds/km: red-headed woodpecker, red-bellied woodpecker, downy woodpecker, blue jay, American crow, American robin, and eastern meadowlark.

Basin, Laurance and Yensen (1985) also could not demonstrate a relationship between rainfall (and assumed seed availability) and winter sparrow abundance. Elmer Finck (personal communication) has observed that tree sparrows, even though foraging in open grassland, prefer to be near shrub vegetation. Such vegetation is, of course, scarce on annually burned watersheds, and thus this species chooses to forage on unburned watersheds, even though total seed availability as well as detectability might be lower. Proximity to shrubs may be related to the accessibility of a refuge for escape from avian predators (Pulliam and Mills 1977; Grubb and Greenwald 1982).

For burned prairie, the only other species recorded at least 20 percent of the time is the rodent-feeding northern harrier. In unburned prairie, woody vegetation attracts a greater diversity, but only ground-feeding insectivorous northern flickers and small, bark-gleaning black-capped chickadees have been observed at least half of the time.

Dickcissels

Frequently on guided tours across the prairie I show native Kansans their first dickcissel, even though it is the most abundant of the grass-dependent core species on the prairie and even more common in fallowed farmland undergoing secondary succession. These folks usually respond that they had often seen the bird before but had thought it to be a baby eastern meadowlark! This response really is not too surprising, since both species present a brown-streaked cryptically patterned backside and a yellow breast with very noticeable black markings on the throat or breast. This black and yellow pattern is presented by no other tallgrass prairie species, although the common yellowthroat offers a variation on this theme. The pattern is repeated in horned larks and western meadowlarks that dominate the shortgrass prairies of western Kansas and the agricultural lands that mimic this habitat and, to a degree, in chestnut-collared longspurs in the northern prairie-pothole region. McCown's longspurs (*Calcarius mccownii*) have the pattern but are gray-white rather than yellow, perhaps in deference to the general hue of the arid shortgrass plains in which they breed. Some open-country buntings in Eurasia have this pattern, but the most striking example in the Eastern Hemisphere is an African pipit with a plumage that matches that of the meadowlark almost stripe for stripe and patch for patch, even though they are quite distantly related. There must be some aspect of the grassland habitat that selects

44

for the evolution of this convergence in plumage pattern among these species. But no one knows what this might be.

There also is a convergence in mating patterns among grassland birds, especially if I include the wet grasslands called marshes, in that many of these species are polygynous (that is, a male is simultaneously mated to more than one female). We do understand something about the derivation of this similarity. One might suspect that this mating system is a reflection of an imbalance in the sex ratio, but this is not true; usually numbers of males and females in these populations are equal. Rather it depends upon the spatial heterogeneity of the habitat in which some males defend territories that are of higher quality than territories of other males. The result is that the males with better territories attract and develop pair bonds with more than one female.

For the dickcissel this difference in territory quality is a function of the vegetation's providing suitable sites in which the female can build her nest. It is not a result of a difference in food resources between territories, since food appears not to limit tallgrass prairie breeding bird populations, and in the case of the dickcissel, the female frequently gathers food for her young wherever it can most easily be found, regardless of the boundaries of the male's well-defined and actively defended territory. In fact, food is so readily available that the male takes no part at all in feeding young; it is such an easy task that his mate can do it all.

Female dickcissels seek out the best nest sites. If a particular male is defending a territory with several suitable sites, he will attract several females. Other males defending territories with fewer sites may attract only one mate. And some males remain bachelors, never attracting a mate. It appears that the aspects of the vegetation that are most important to the nesting female are its depth and density. Males with territories containing a greater volume of forbs and grasses attract more females because the nest must be placed deep within the vegetation. This covert placement moderates daily fluctuations in nest temperature and especially protects the nest from the heat of a summer's afternoon. At nests in which Gilbert Blankespoor artificially opened up the vegetation, the female had to spend so much of her time shading the young from direct sunlight that she spent too little time gathering food. Although the young did fledge, they left the nest at a lower weight than young from more-protected nests. Although not demonstrated, Gil assumed that these less well fed fledglings would have a lower survival rate during the critical period just after leaving the nest.

Males who do not attract females are not condemned to celibacy. By carefully watching males from sunrise to sunset, Leigh Schartz discovered that males occasionally leave their territories, flying over the horizon and out of sight. The amount of time a male spends in these distant flights each day is a function of the number of his mates. Mateless males do it the most; males with several females do it the least. (Elmer Finck was able to confirm this conclusion by demonstrating that Konza Prairie males, who are never more than bigamists, spend more of their time in distant flight than oldfield males who are better mated.) These are probably exploratory flights through which males discover alternative sites in which competition for space is less intense and where they might have a better chance of carving out a territory with suitable nest sites and hence a better chance of attracting a female. As a result bachelors do not maintain their territories very long; they leave after about 12 days of unrewarded advertisement of their availability.

Once I was able to follow a bachelor who had remained mateless for two weeks, but then moved just 200 m and was able to wedge himself into a patch of suitable habitat, compressing the territories of adjacent males. Within a few days he attracted a mate. Males that do attract several mates during one breeding season will return to the same territory the next breeding season. Less-successful mated males will return to the same general area but move their territory the next year. The data do not significantly support the expectation that in their new, supposedly better territory they will attract more mates; but the mean number of females for the subsequent year is greater.

I do have a record of six dickcissel eggs in a single nest, but normally the female lays four pale blue eggs in a grassy nest that preferably is placed in a stout forb but may also be in grass clumps. It is rare, however, to find a nest on Konza Prairie with just dickcissel eggs, since these birds suffer intense social parasitism by the brown-headed cowbird. In May and early June almost all dickcissel nests contain at least one cowbird egg, and the proportion of parasitized nests does not drop below 50 percent until mid-July, when the cowbirds' breeding season begins to wane.

I once found a dickcissel nest in an oldfield habitat with seven cowbird eggs, but two or three cowbird eggs in a nest are more common. This number indicates that more than one cowbird female is using the same host nest. When the cowbird lays its egg in another species' nest, it usually removes one of the host's eggs. Heavy parasitism results in an average loss of two dickcissel eggs per nest in May and June and one egg in late July. Thus cowbird parasitism depresses productivity of dickcissels by almost 30 percent. This impact, coupled with snake predation, means the chance of a prairie nest producing young dickcissels is only about 15 in 100.

If a female is successful in fledging young after about 26 days of nest life, she will continue to care for them for another two weeks. Even if she initially began nesting in early June, there is not enough time for a second brood. Dickcissels, like all birds, are energy dependent, and it appears that the migratory schedule of the species has evolved in response to the seasonal changes in the environment: changes in photoperiod that affect its ability to gather food and the moderation in temperature that allows it to direct energy into reproductive activities rather than thermoregulation.

Males abandon their territories in August, often before their mates have completed their reproductive chores. They leave the prairie and gather in the rank vegetation along streamsides and fallow fields to undergo the fall molt; eventually they are joined by females and juveniles. Here they take advantage of the abundance of insects, gorging themselves almost to the point of obesity, putting on fat for the autumnal migration. Birds continue to collect from adjacent breeding habitats until these molting and fattening flocks often number over 50 birds. Then on a September morning they are gone, departing during the night toward their primary wintering range on the llanos of Venezuela in northern South America. Studies of their physiology indicate that even though temperatures are still pleasant and food is still abundant, the birds leave just in time. If they lingered, the decreasing day length and the slowly sinking temperatures of autumn would not allow them sufficient energy surplus to put on the necessary fat to initiate their migratory journey.

The return of the dickcissels in spring is also a function of the interaction of day length and temperature. Even though they could survive quite well all year long on their tropical wintering grounds, at least in terms of the permissiveness of the climate, increasing day length and moderate temperatures of the north temperate spring and summer offer a surplus of energy that then can be channeled into reproduction. Thus there is an advantage to be gained in migrating north. Males appear in early May, filling habitat space in fallow land and hay fields first but then spilling out into the tallgrass prairie. Here they establish their territories through incessant singing, stopping from time to time to aggressively chase intruding males in a twisting turning flight that sometimes crashes into the ground with an explosion of feathers. Females return about a week later to again select the territory with the best nest sites so that partners can be chosen and the dance can continue once again, as it has for thousands of years.

There is concern, however, that the future of the dickcissel as the most abundant territorial bird in the tallgrass prairie is in jeopardy. As is usually the case, the problem arises from the detrimental impact of human activities on the success of a bird that has evolved through the ages in the absence of human interference. Primevally dickcissels wintering on the llanos of northern South America probably lived by gaining their energy income from the seeds of the native plants. Now, in Venezuela, for example, dickcissels feed on the seeds of such cultivated plants as grain sorghums and rice. Indeed, they are an agricultural pest, foraging across the countryside in flocks numbering in the thousands and seriously affecting agricultural production.

Steve Fretwell suggested that this shift in diet favors males: They are larger than females and therefore can more effectively handle the larger seeds of domesticated plants, whereas smaller females must continue to forage on wild seeds. But since the wild seed crop is being depleted by the conversion of wildland into cropland, females suffer reduced food availability and hence lower survival. Upon their return to temperate breeding grounds, the reduced numbers of females are reflected in reduced nest densities that result in heavy parasitism by cowbirds, which in turn reduces fecundity, resulting in even fewer females. Such a positive feedback system eventually leads to annihilation. The roadside breeding-bird survey conducted by the U.S. Fish and Wildlife Service throughout North America has indicated a significant decline of dickcissels in recent years—data that support this prediction of doom. Although Fretwell's scenario is more biologically elegant in its dependence on differential survival and productivity, the measured decrease in population may be due to a more direct cause. In order to control the depredation of crops by wintering dickcissels, biocides have been used to eliminate these agricultural pests.

3 Forest Communities

As has been observed elsewhere in the Great Plains (Faanes 1984), wooded areas attract an assemblage of bird species quite out of proportion to the coverage of the habitat in the region. In 1939 only 4.5 percent of the total acreage of Konza Prairie was forested, and the most recent estimate (1985) indicated that about 7 percent was covered by trees (Knight 1991)—yet this habitat is associated with 50 percent of the total species of birds known from the site (Fig. 9). These tree-dominated communities are arrayed parallel to the lower stream channels of Kings and Shane creeks like the choir galleries on either side of the apse in Gothic cathedrals and extend up the watersheds into the interior of the upland prairie, varying in width from 300 m to 10 m. Forested fingers in the drier declivities of draws become discontinuous, disjunct patches developing in association with perennial springs; these patches are separated from other similar tree islands by scattered tree lines or intervening prairie. Abrams (1986) recognized four forest stands along a continuum from mesic to more xeric. On the basis of Abrams's analysis and habitat selection of breeding birds (Mikesell 1988), the gallery forest can be divided into two subgroups: the gallery forest proper and the attenuated gallery forest.

THE GALLERY FOREST

The gallery forest includes the two more mesic of Abrams's stands. The most mesic association occurs on sites with low slope and soil with high silt content—that is, the lower flood-plain of creeks. The codominant species are bur oak and hack-berry with chinquapin oak and elm as subdominants. Additional tree species include green ash, honey locust, black walnut, box elder, and mulberry. Bur oaks have a minimum diameter breast high (DBH) of 40 centimeters (cm) and a minimum age of 70 years, whereas mature hackberry trees range in age from 23 to 57 years and in size from 10 to 40 cm DBH. There is little reproduction by oaks in the shade of their canopy, but hackberry and elm are reproducing and will eventually replace the oaks as dominants. The shrub stratum is poorly developed, with no buckbrush, and there is no redbud in the understory. This stand grades into the next, in which bur oak becomes the sole dominant species with chinquapin oak, hackberry, and elm as subdominants. Sycamore, locust, green ash, and walnut also occur, and redbud and buckbrush make their appearance.

Abrams's (1985) study of fire scars indicated that in the Kings Creek drainage, fire burned into the interior of the gallery forest about every 20 years; fire incidence in Shane Creek was more frequent—about every 11 years. An analysis by Abrams (1988) on gallery forest sites subjected to annual burning revealed that fire reduced the number and percentage cover of both tree saplings and shrubs like buckbrush and rough-leaved dogwood but did not directly affect mature individuals of the dominant tree species. He suggested, however, that persistent annual burning in gallery forest would prevent the succession from bur oak to hackberry and eventually could convert gallery forest into oak savanna. With continued fire and its inhibition of recruitment of woody plants and the eventual death of the mature oaks, these oak savannas would be replaced by prairie. This may have been the presettlement condition. Early land surveys in the mid-nineteenth century suggest that prior to development of agrarian and urban communities by settlers from the eastern United States and Europe, forests were "mere ribbons along the water courses." During the subsequent years of active fire suppression, however, the forest expanded to its present extent (Reichman 1987).

The gallery forest provides the greatest diversity and abundance of birds of all breeding-bird communities on Konza Prairie, and their numbers are the most stable from year to year, having a coefficient of variation of only 16.2 (Fig. 3). Although populations of the woody-dependent species in grassland habitats as well as the grass-dependent core species in annually burned watersheds are correlated with March soil moisture (Zimmerman 1992), the relationship is not significant for the abundance of gallery forest birds. This independence certainly reflects the downstream position of the gallery forest, which makes it less sensitive to the annual vagaries of rainfall and soil moisture in upland prairie and which in some way contributes to the greater stability of the bird population. Furthermore, the relative permanence of the above-ground biomass of trees and shrubs provides a certain degree of habitat continuity during short-term perturbations in climate and food supply.

Bird populations in the gallery forest at Konza Prairie also are relatively more stable than those of birds in an Illinois forest over a 50–year period during a time when the characteristics of that habitat were significantly affected by the die-off of the American elm (Kendeigh 1982). In the Illinois woodlot, the mean number of species (27.9) was similar to that of the Konza Prairie gallery forest (30.6), but the coefficient of variation of species richness was twice as great (22.4 compared to 10.8). The abundance measure of birds in the Illinois woods is not comparable to the gallery forest, since the methods were quite different. Yet the mean of 165 territorial males per 24 hectares (ha) (Kendeigh 1982:Appendix 1) had a coefficient of variation equal to 101— over six times greater than that of the relative abundance of birds based on transect data in the Konza Prairie gallery forest.

Breeding-bird survey data for Kansas (S. Droege, unpublished) can also be compared to the populations of gallery forest birds on Konza Prairie during the period 1981 through 1990 (Table 5). Again, using a sign test on runs, bobwhite, field sparrow, and rufous-sided towhee each show significant trends from low to high over this 10-year period. These three species also similarly increased in unburned prairie over these years. Although not significant, positive trends are suggested for yellow warbler, black-and-white warbler, and northern cardinal. Only the increase in towhees reflects the pattern in Kansas. There are no significant negative trends in the gallery forest data, but the data suggest decreases in eastern wood-pewee, blue-gray gnatcatcher, and brown-headed cowbird. Of these patterns, that for the gnatcatcher reflects the Kansas trend.

The Konza Prairie gallery forest and the tabulation for Kansas have 31 species in common, of which 18 species (58 percent) share the same trends or lack of trends. A similar comparison of data from the Hubbard-Brook forest in New Hampshire and breeding-bird survey data for that state (Holmes and Sherry 1988) showed 63 percent of the species had the same trends (or lack of trends). The effect of this difference in scale (from local stand to the whole state) in these pairs of data sets is similar in both regions and suggests a degree of error that should be expected if it is necessary to extrapolate trend data from a local stand typifying the region to a wider area.

Of the breeding species in the gallery forest, 38 percent are permanent residents. Among summer residents, over half (52 percent) winter in the neotropics, and the remainder stay within the temperate zone (Table 6). No trends in the gallery forest data are related to migratory status or contranuptial region. As Robbins et al. (1989) concluded, it is the neotropical migrants that winter within the forest interior that have shown the greater decline in numbers on breeding-bird survey routes compared to species wintering in scrub. Of the neotropical migrants that breed in the gallery forest of Konza Prairie, only the great crested flycatcher, red-eyed vireo, black-and-white warbler, and Kentucky warbler are forest interior wintering species, and only the flycatcher is a principal member of the Konza avifauna. Thus the

53

TABLE 5 Abundance Trends (1980–1991) on June Transects in Konza Prairie Forest Species Compared to Kansas Patterns[a]

	Konza Prairie		
	Gallery Forest	Attenuated Forest	Kansas
Ring-necked pheasant	ns	—	ns
Northern bobwhite	increase	ns	ns
Mourning dove	ns	ns	decrease
Yellow-billed cuckoo	ns	decrease	decrease
Common nighthawk	—	ns	—
Belted kingfisher	ns	—	ns
Red-headed woodpecker	ns	decrease	decrease
Red-bellied woodpecker	ns	ns	increase
Downy woodpecker	ns	—	ns
Hairy woodpecker	ns	—	increase
Northern flicker	ns	decrease	decrease
Eastern wood-pewee	decrease?	—	ns
Eastern phoebe	ns	ns	ns
Great crested flycatcher	ns	ns	ns
Blue jay	ns	ns	ns
American crow	ns	ns	increase
Black-capped chickadee	ns	ns	ns
Tufted titmouse	ns	ns	ns
White-breasted nuthatch	ns	ns	ns
Bewick's wren	—	ns	—
House wren	ns	ns	ns
Blue-gray gnatcatcher	decrease?	—	decrease
Eastern bluebird	ns	ns	increase
American robin	ns	—	ns
Brown thrasher	ns	ns	ns
Red-eyed vireo	ns	—	ns
Louisiana waterthrush	ns	—	—
Summer tanager	ns	—	—
Northern cardinal	increase?	ns	ns
Red-breasted grosbeak	ns	—	ns
Indigo bunting	ns	ns	ns
Dickcissel	—	ns	decrease
Field sparrow	increase	ns	ns
Grasshopper sparrow	—	ns	decrease
Eastern meadowlark	—	ns	decrease
Common grackle	ns	—	ns
Brown-headed cowbird	decrease?	ns	ns

Northern oriole	ns	—	ns
American goldfinch	—	ns	ns
Yellow warbler[b]	increase?	—	ns
Black-and-white warbler[b]	increase?	—	—
Rufous-sided towhee[b]	increase	—	increase

ns = no significant trend. — = no data.

[a]Data for Konza Prairie species exclude raptors, prairie-chickens, swallows, and species that have occurred in fewer than 50 percent of the years on June transects.

[b]Species recorded in fewer than 50 percent of the years, but all records in the last five years.

TABLE 6 Annual Species Richness and Seasonal Status on June Transects for All Gallery Forest Species[a]

		Resident Both Summer and	Summer Resident	Winter Range of Summer Residents	
Year	Number	Winter	Only	North Temperate Zone	Neotropics
1981	30	13	17	7	10
1982	31	13	18	9	9
1983	30	11	19	10	9
1984	28	10	18	10	8
1985	24	10	14	7	7
1986	30	11	19	9	10
1987	36	14	22	10	12
1988	34	11	23	12	11
1989	30	12	18	8	10
1990	33	12	21	8	13
mean	30.6	11.7	18.9	9.0	9.9
S.E.	1.05	0.42	0.82	0.49	0.57
C.V.	10.8	11.4	13.8	17.4	18.1
%		38	62	48	52

[a]Excluded are species occurring in fewer than 20 percent of the years on June transects.

absence of declining trends for neotropical migrants in the Konza data is to be expected, at least for now.

A guild is a group of species that depends upon the same class of environmental resources and employs similar ways of exploiting them (Root 1967). Although a taxonomically diverse grouping, guilds are helpful in describing the ecological relation-

55

ships among the species in a community. Based on the analyses of Willson (1974) and Holmes et al. (1979), the birds of the gallery forest that have occurred on at least half of the annual transects (included in Fig. 15) have been categorized into eight guilds (Table 7). There are no significant differences among the mean coefficients of variation for relative abundances of species in various guilds. No guild is especially more vulnerable to variations in resources than any other. The subcanopy insectivores and sally insectivores are similar in their variability, as are the three ground-shrub feeding guilds. Gray (1989) showed that densities of sally insectivores and densities of insectivores in the canopy (tufted titmouse), subcanopy (black-capped chickadee), and ground-shrub stratum (Louisiana waterthrush) are correlated with the biomass of the emergent insects from Kings Creek. Perhaps, therefore, timing of food availability for an array of species in a variety of different guilds produces the similarity in their annual variabilities. As Willson (1974) reported, there is considerable overlap in the areas of territories between species belonging to the same guild and no consistent morphological differences among these species, suggesting that competition has not driven species into mutually exclusive niches. Furthermore, as Holmes et al. (1979) concluded, the major factors separating birds into guilds are the physical structure of the habitat (e.g., ground, canopy, and tree bark) and the morphology of the plant species (e.g., branching patterns, leaf arrangements) rather than any special differences in food resources.

Winter communities in all habitats have fewer species and lower relative abundances than summer communities (Figs. 2 and 3). This is to be expected in mid-latitudes within the interior of North America. Even though the numbers of species and relative abundances are distinctly different between the seasons in a particular community, ranges of these values across communities are quite similar between the seasons (Fig. 16). What is striking in this figure is the difference in the ranges of coefficients of variation between seasons. There is a considerably greater range

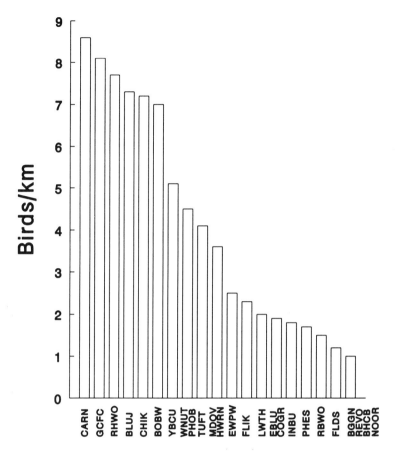

Figure 15. Mean relative abundances (birds/km, N = 10) of species, 1981–1990, on June transects in gallery forest, except for raptors and species occurring in fewer than 20 percent of the years. BGGN = blue-gray gnatcatcher, BHCB = brown-headed cowbird, BLUJ = blue jay, BOBW = northern bobwhite, CARN = northern cardinal, CHIK = black-capped chickadee, COGR = common grackle, EBLU = eastern bluebird, EWPW = eastern wood-pewee, FLDS = field sparrow, FLIK = northern flicker, GCFC = great crested flycatcher, HWRN = house wren, INBU = indigo bunting, LWTH = Louisiana waterthrush, MDOV = mourning dove, NOOR = northern oriole, PHES = ring-necked pheasant, PHOB = eastern phoebe, RBWO = red-bellied woodpecker, REVO = red-eyed vireo, RHWO = red-headed woodpecker, TUFT = tufted titmouse, WNUT = white-breasted nuthatch, YBCU = yellow-billed cuckoo. Species with mean values < 1.0 birds/km: great blue heron, green-backed heron, black-billed cuckoo, downy woodpecker, hairy woodpecker, eastern kingbird, American crow, American robin, gray catbird, brown thrasher, European starling, warbling vireo, northern parula, yellow warbler, black-and-white warbler, Kentucky warbler, summer tanager, rose-breasted grosbeak, rufous-sided towhee, American goldfinch.

TABLE 7 Guild Organization in the Gallery Forest with Coefficients of
Variation and Relative Abundances on June Transects[a]

	C.V.	Birds/Km ± S.E.[b]
Ground stratum herbivore		
Mourning dove	85	3.6 ± 0.98
Ground and shrub strata omnivore		
Northern cardinal	25	8.6 ± 0.67
Blue jay	34	7.3 ± 0.78
Northern bobwhite	51	7.0 ± 1.13
Common grackle	143	1.9 ± 0.86
Ring-necked pheasant	50	1.7 ± 0.26
Brown-headed cowbird	114	1.0 ± 0.38
American crow	150	0.8 ± 0.38
Brown thrasher	105	0.6 ± 0.20
American robin	78	0.5 ± 0.12
mean	83	
Ground and shrub strata insectivore		
House wren	89	3.6 ± 1.01
Louisiana waterthrush	70	2.0 ± 0.45
Field sparrow	88	1.2 ± 0.32
mean	82	
Subcanopy insectivore		
Black-capped chickadee	59	7.2 ± 1.33
Yellow-billed cuckoo	37	5.1 ± 0.60
Eastern bluebird	64	1.9 ± 0.38
Indigo bunting	54	1.8 ± 0.32
Blue-gray gnatcatcher	122	1.0 ± 0.38
mean	67	
Canopy insectivore		
Tufted titmouse	46	4.1 ± 0.59
Northern oriole	144	1.0 ± 0.48
Red-eyed vireo	74	1.0 ± 0.24
Rose-breasted grosbeak	67	0.7 ± 0.14
Summer tanager	110	0.6 ± 0.19
mean	88	
Sally insectivore		
Great crested flycatcher	51	8.1 ± 1.29
Eastern phoebe	52	4.5 ± 0.75
Eastern wood-pewee	105	2.5 ± 0.82
mean	69	
Bark insectivore/omnivore		
Red-headed woodpecker	38	7.7 ± 0.93
White-breasted nuthatch	59	4.5 ± 0.84

Northern flicker	64	2.3 ± 0.46
Red-bellied woodpecker	86	1.5 ± 0.40
Downy woodpecker	141	0.8 ± 0.36
Hairy woodpecker	86	0.4 ± 0.10
mean	79	
Aquatic piscivore		
Belted kingfisher	112	1.2 ± 0.42

[a]Excluded are species seen in fewer than 50 percent of the years on June transects.

[b]Listed in descending order of abundance.

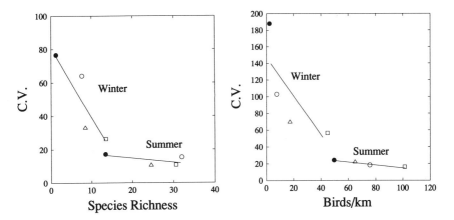

Figure 16. Relationships between species richness (number of species) and relative abundance (birds/km) and their coefficients of variation (C.V.) in summer and winter in major habitats (solid circle = annually burned grassland, open circle = unburned grassland, triangle = attenuated gallery forest, square = gallery forest). The coefficients of variation for both species richness and relative abundance are very similar between habitats during the summer, reflecting little change in their suitabilities from year to year. In winter, however, annual variation for both measures is higher and increases with decreasing structure of the community from gallery forest to annually burned grassland.

across the various communities in the annual variability within communities during the winter compared to the very narrow range of variation common to all communities in summer. Summer birds are largely territorial, a social system that generates stability within communities from year to year. Furthermore, environmental resources during the breeding season are usually   59 adequate and frequently more than adequate. Thus summer variation is lower. The range in the coefficients of variation across the communities is also tightly clumped, suggesting that there is little difference between these habitats in summer-to-summer suitability.

In winter, however, climatic conditions are harsher. Winter resources are more variable from year to year, being dependent upon timing of summer rains that result in good seed set and upon the effect of spring freezes and summer droughts on fruit crop. These factors lead not only to higher values for coefficients of variation in winter populations in all communities but also to a greater disparity between communities. The least-structured annually burned grassland experiences the greatest variation, whereas the most-structured gallery forest is the most stable. Furthermore, a large share of the winter population in the gallery forest is composed of permanent residents (87 percent of total individuals), with a very small contribution from species arriving as migrants to winter in this habitat (Table 8). There are few permanent residents in winter grasslands (Fig. 14): only 26 percent of the total individuals in unburned grasslands and none in annually burned grasslands. Grassland communities are therefore dependent upon a whole set of off-site factors that determine sizes of populations that will arrive to spend the winter and hence are highly variable from year to year.

A total of 22 species has been observed on January transects within the gallery forest in at least 20 percent of the years from 1982 through 1991 (Fig. 17). Mean species richness is 13.5 ± 1.1, and relative abundance averages 44.8 ± 8.01 birds/km (Fig. 2). This habitat supports the highest diversity and density of all winter habitats on Konza Prairie.

The guild relationships of the species occurring during winter (Table 9) are simpler than during the foliage-dominated breeding season when insects are active. Only four guilds (the bark insectivores/omnivores, the acorn feeders, the frugivores, and the ground stratum seed eaters) are apparent, although the

TABLE 8 Annual Species Richness and Seasonal Status for Forest Birds on January Transects[a]

	Gallery Forest			Attenuated Gallery Forest		
Year	Number	Resident Both Summer and Winter	Winter Residents Only	Number	Resident Both Summer and Winter	Winter Residents Only
1982	15	12	3	12	10	2
1983	15	11	4	7	7	0
1984	11	10	1	9	8	1
1985	9	7	2	6	6	0
1986	18	16	2	9	8	1
1987	14	10	4	12	11	1
1988	14	12	2	7	6	1
1989	19	16	3	11	10	1
1990	8	7	1	3	3	0
1991	12	11	1	9	9	0
mean	13.5	11.2	2.3	8.5	7.5	0.7
S.E.	1.13	0.98	0.37	0.90	0.76	0.21
C.V.	26.4	27.5	50.4	33.4	30.7	96.4
%		83	17		92	8

[a]Excluded are species occurring in fewer than 20 percent of the years on January transects.

bark insectivores/omnivores can be divided into bark-gleaning and bark-drilling subsets. It comes as no surprise that this guild is the most stable: The five bark gleaners have an average coefficient of variation equal to 85 and the bark drillers average 90. Five species in this guild form the core of winter mixed-species flocks in the forest (red-bellied woodpecker, downy woodpecker, black-capped chickadee, tufted titmouse, and white-breasted nuthatch), and these species have the lowest mean measure of annual variation (C.V. = 70). The numbers of acorn feeders are correlated with mast crop production (Finck 1986), and in spite of occasional failures in bur oak mast, acorn feeders are the next most stable guild (C.V. = 92). Of the three species in this guild, the red-bellied woodpecker has a wide feeding niche that includes wood-boring insects; hence these birds can overwinter in

61

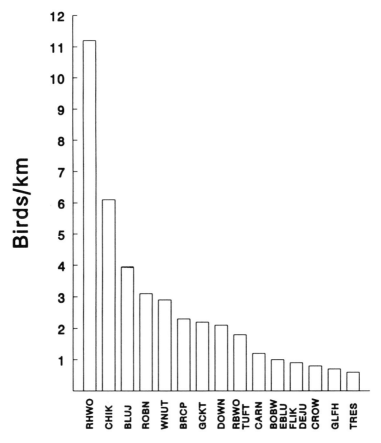

Figure 17. Mean relative abundances (birds/km, N = 10) of species, 1982–1991, on January transects in gallery forest, except for raptors and species occurring in fewer than 20 percent of the years. BLU-J = blue jay, BOBW = northern bobwhite, BRCP = brown creeper, CARN = northern cardinal, CHIK = black-capped chickadee, CROW = American crow, DEJU = dark-eyed junco, DOWN = downy woodpecker, EBLU = eastern bluebird, FLIK = northern flicker, GCKT = golden-crowned kinglet, GLFH = American goldfinch, RBWO = red-bellied woodpecker, RHWO = red-headed woodpecker, ROBN = American robin, TRES = American tree sparrow, TUFT = tufted titmouse, WNUT = white-breasted nuthatch. The following species had means < 0.5 birds/km: belted kingfisher, hairy wood-pecker.

TABLE 9 Guild Organization in the Gallery Forest with Coefficients of
Variation and Relative Abundances on January Transects[a]

	C.V.	Birds/Km ± S.E.[b]
BARK INSECTIVORES/OMNIVORES		
Drillers		
Downy woodpecker	59	2.1 ± 0.39
Red-bellied woodpecker (in part)	86	1.8 ± 0.50
Northern flicker (in part)	97	0.9 ± 0.26
Hairy woodpecker	116	0.4 ± 0.14
mean	90	
Gleaners		
Black-capped chickadee	62	6.1 ± 1.19
White-breasted nuthatch	61	2.9 ± 0.56
Brown creeper	127	2.3 ± 0.92
Golden-crowned kinglet	96	2.3 ± 0.67
Tufted titmouse	80	1.8 ± 0.46
mean	85	
ACORN FEEDERS		
Red-headed woodpecker	83	11.2 ± 2.97
Blue jay	106	3.8 ± 1.29
Red-bellied woodpecker (in part)	86	1.6 ± 0.50
mean	92	
FRUGIVORES		
American robin	219	3.1 ± 2.14
Eastern bluebird	135	1.0 ± 0.42
Northern flicker (in part)	97	0.9 ± 0.26
mean	150	
GROUND STRATUM SEED EATERS		
Northern cardinal	162	1.2 ± 0.60
American crow	171	0.8 ± 0.43
mean	166	

[a]Excluded are species seen in fewer than 50 percent of the years on January
transects.

[b]Listed in descending order of abundance.

the habitat in low mast years (Williams and Batzli 1979). Blue
jays also have a wide niche. When acorns are scarce, perhaps the
jays move out of the gallery forest to feed on seeds that are best
discovered in association with agricultural areas, or perhaps
they migrate out of the area. Other studies that related numbers

63

of winter jays to acorn abundances produced ambiguous results (see Hickey and Brittingham 1991). Most of the red-headed woodpeckers migrate when the bur oak crop fails. The frugivores (whose food supply is largely dependent upon whether the hackberry flowers were frozen in the previous spring) and the ground-feeding seed eaters have the most year-to-year variation. The latter guild also was present at the lowest relative abundance, a pattern that is opposite to that observed in forested habitats well within the eastern deciduous forest biome where this guild is dominant in winter (Blake 1987).

THE ATTENUATED GALLERY FOREST

The attenuated gallery forest comprises the two driest stands in Abrams's (1986) survey. The gallery forest always lies below the Cottonwood limestone formation (Jewett 1941; refer to Fig. 21), whereas the attenuated gallery forest lies both below and above this prominent outcrop. At the lower elevations this association is formed by bur oak and chinquapin oak as codominants, with elm and redbud as subdominants. The oaks are largely over 70 years of age, 20 to 30 cm DBH, and not reproducing greatly, whereas elm and redbud are less than 34 years old and reproducing well. Hackberry is still present but in low frequency; green ash, honey locust, walnut, and mulberry also are present. The shrub stratum is well developed, with rough-leaved dogwood the primary species. At the highest, most xeric sites, chinquapin oak is the dominant species, with bur oak, redbud, and elm as subdominants. Although walnut and mulberry are still present, there is no hackberry. Again oaks are the oldest—some at least 52 years of age; elms and redbuds are less than 38 years old. Redbuds have the greatest coverage of any of these stands and are reproducing quite well.

Killingbeck (1988) analyzed the soil microhabitats of the two oak species and demonstrated that bur oak is associated with high concentrations of phosphate phosphorus, whereas chinquapin oak occurs on soils of lower fertility. He hypothesized that this distribution is an indirect effect of fire. On the one hand, lower-fertility soil would produce lower fuel loads and hence sustain fires of lower intensity; on the other hand, fires invading gallery forest on soils that were more fertile would be more intense because of the greater amount of fuel. Since saplings of chinquapin oak are more susceptible to fire than bur oak saplings, chinquapin oaks are restricted to sites of lower fuel production—that is, sites of lower fertility.

The interface between two habitats such as forest and prairie, called edge habitat, is characterized by high species richness. Although the attenuated gallery forest is clearly an edge habitat, species richness and the relative abundance of birds found there on June transects are exceeded by both the gallery forest and unburned grassland communities (Fig. 2). Of the species that have been observed during at least 20 percent of the years (Fig. 18), 84 percent are shared with the gallery forest. If the coefficients of variation for the 18 species that have been present on at least half of the June transects in both habitats are compared, the greater mean coefficient of variation in the attenuated gallery forest ($\bar{x} = 86.8$) is significantly different (Student's $t = 2.05$, $df = 34$, $P < 0.05$) from the mean in the gallery forest ($\bar{x} = 64.0$). This difference is possibly explained by the greater vulnerability to drought of the attenuated gallery forest. The relative abundances of birds in attenuated gallery forest on June transects are significantly correlated with March soil moisture values, as are those in grassland communities (Zimmerman 1992), whereas gallery forest bird populations are independent. This is to be expected from the topographical position of the attenuated forest higher in the watersheds.

Mikesell's (1988) analysis indicated that within the attenuated gallery forest species are ordered by elevation in the watershed. Species like northern oriole, house wren, black-capped chickadee, northern cardinal, and great crested flycatcher occur in habitats more similar to the gallery forest; species like brown

65

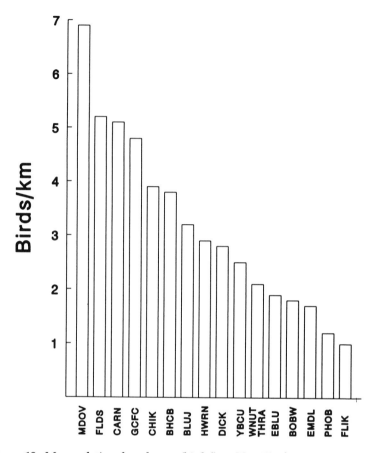

Figure 18. Mean relative abundances (birds/km, N = 10) of species, 1981–1990, on June transects in attenuated gallery forest, except for raptors and species occurring in fewer than 20 percent of the years. BHCB = brown-headed cowbird, BLUJ = blue jay, BOBW = northern bobwhite, CARN = northern cardinal, CHIK = black-capped chickadee, DICK = dickcissel, EBLU = eastern bluebird, EMDL = eastern meadowlark, FLDS = field sparrow, FLIK = northern flicker, GCFC = great crested flycatcher, HWRN = house wren, MDOV = mourning dove, PHOB = eastern phoebe, THRA = brown thrasher, WNUT = white-breasted nuthatch, YBCU = yellow-billed cuckoo. Species with means < 1.0 birds/km: ring-necked pheasant, black-billed cuckoo, common nighthawk, red-headed woodpecker, red-bellied woodpecker, downy woodpecker, hairy woodpecker, eastern wood-pewee, American crow, tufted titmouse, Bewick's wren, blue-gray gnatcatcher, gray catbird, Bell's vireo, warbling vireo, red-eyed vireo, black-and-white warbler, Louisiana waterthrush, Kentucky warbler, summer tanager, rose-breasted grosbeak, indigo bunting, rufous-sided towhee, lark sparrow, grasshopper sparrow, northern oriole, American goldfinch.

thrasher, rufous-sided towhee, and field sparrow, however, were shown to be characteristic of the ecotonal interface with the rock outcrop shrub and the unburned grassland communities. Thus in the analysis of guild arrangement it is necessary to divide the community into a grassy patch subgroup and a shrub-tree patch subgroup (Table 10). Nine guilds are present, with the ground and shrub strata insectivores recognized in each of the subgroups. There are no significant differences between the coefficients of variation for these guilds or with comparable guilds in the gallery forest, even though the comparison of the communities as a whole shows greater variability in the less-structured, more water-dependent attenuated gallery forest.

This vulnerability of the attenuated gallery forest is also shown in populations of the yellow-billed cuckoo, red-headed woodpecker, and northern flicker—species that have been stable in the gallery forest but show significantly decreasing trends in the attenuated gallery forest (Table 5). This latter pattern, furthermore, is comparable to the status of these three species throughout the state.

As in gallery forest, the proportion of species that occur during both the summer and winter composes over a third of the community, but the percentage of summer residents that are neotropical migrants is less (Table 11).

Transects during January in the attenuated gallery forest have noted 18 species that have been recorded on at least 20 percent of the years (Fig. 19). The mean species richness, however, is 8.5 ± 0.90 (Fig. 2), with permanent residents making up the greatest proportion (92 percent) of any of the winter communities on Konza Prairie. The annual variability of the permanent residents is only a third of that calculated for the birds that are present only as winter residents (Table 8). Since hackberry is poorly represented in the attenuated forest, no frugivores are found there except the northern flicker, which probably is depending upon poison ivy as well as shifting into the bark-drilling assemblage of insectivores (Table 12). The low density of bur

TABLE 10 Guild Organization in the Attenuated Gallery Forest with
Coefficients of Variation and Relative Abundances on June Transects[a]

	C.V.	Birds/Km ± S.E.[b]
GRASSY PATCH SUBGROUP		
Ground and shrub strata insectivores		
Field sparrow	66	5.2 ± 1.08
Brown-headed cowbird	56	3.8 ± 0.67
Dickcissel	33	2.8 ± 0.29
Eastern meadowlark	77	1.7 ± 0.41
Grasshopper sparrow	136	0.9 ± 0.39
mean	74	
SHRUB-TREE PATCH SUBGROUP		
Ground-feeding herbivores		
Mourning dove	41	6.9 ± 0.90
Ground and shrub strata omnivores		
Northern cardinal	44	5.1 ± 0.71
Blue jay	42	3.2 ± 0.42
Brown thrasher	65	2.1 ± 0.43
Northern bobwhite	90	1.8 ± 0.50
American crow	123	0.7 ± 0.27
mean	73	
Ground and shrub strata insectivores		
House wren	74	2.9 ± 0.61
Bewick's wren	130	0.9 ± 0.38
mean	102	
Ground and shrub strata herbivores		
American goldfinch	128	0.6 ± 0.25
Subcanopy insectivores		
Black-capped chickadee	79	3.9 ± 0.98
Yellow-billed cuckoo	38	2.5 ± 0.30
Eastern bluebird	91	1.9 ± 0.55
Indigo bunting	141	0.8 ± 0.34
mean	87	
Canopy insectivores		
Tufted titmouse	123	0.7 ± 0.27
Sally insectivores		
Great crested flycatcher	46	4.8 ± 0.71
Eastern phoebe	127	1.2 ± 0.46
mean	86	
Aerial insectivores		
Common nighthawk	128	0.6 ± 0.25
Bark insectivores		
White-breasted nuthatch	150	2.1 ± 0.98

Northern flicker	63	1.0 ± 0.20
Red-bellied woodpecker	77	0.9 ± 0.22
Red-headed woodpecker	125	0.8 ± 0.30
mean	104	

[a]Excluded are species seen in fewer than 50 percent of the years on June transects.
[b]Listed in descending order of abundance.

TABLE 11 Annual Species Richness and Seasonal Status on June Transects for Attenuated Gallery Forest Species[a]

| | | Resident Both Summer and | Summer Residents | Wintering Area of Summer Residents | |
Year	Number	Winter	Only	North Temperate Zone	Neotropics
1981	23	8	15	7	8
1982	26	10	16	10	6
1983	29	13	16	9	7
1984	24	9	15	10	5
1985	20	8	12	5	7
1986	24	10	14	8	6
1987	27	10	17	10	7
1988	27	6	21	11	10
1989	22	7	15	10	5
1990	24	9	15	10	5
mean	24.6	9.0	15.6	9.0	6.6
S.E.	0.85	0.62	0.73	0.58	0.50
C.V.	10.9	21.6	14.9	20.3	23.9
%		37	63	58	42

[a]Excluded are species occurring in fewer than 20 percent of the years on June transects.

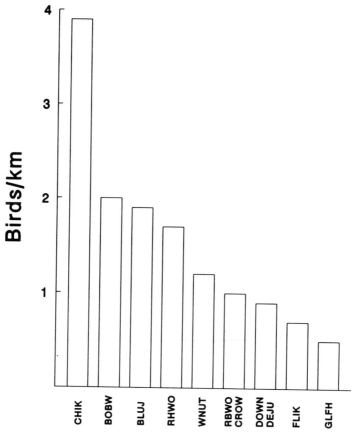

Figure 19. Mean relative abundances (birds/km, N = 10) of species, 1982–1991, on January transects in attenuated gallery forest, except for raptors and species occurring in fewer than 20 percent of the years. BLUJ = blue jay, BOBW = northern bobwhite, CHIK = black-capped chickadee, CROW = American crow, DEJU = dark-eyed junco, DOWN = downy woodpecker, FLIK = northern flicker, GLFH = American goldfinch, RBWO = red-bellied woodpecker, RHWO = red-headed woodpecker, WNUT = white-breasted nuthatch. Species with mean values < 0.5 birds/km: tufted titmouse, eastern bluebird, American robin, northern cardinal, American tree sparrow.

TABLE 12 Guild Organization in the Attenuated Gallery Forest with Coefficients of Variation and Relative Abundances on January Transects[a]

	C.V.	Birds/Km ± S.E.[b]
BARK INSECTIVORES/OMNIVORES		
Drillers		
Red-bellied woodpecker	89	1.0 ± 0.28
Downy woodpecker	66	0.9 ± 0.19
Northern flicker (in part)	98	0.7 ± 0.21
Gleaners		
Black-capped chickadee	116	3.9 ± 1.44
White-breasted nuthatch	111	1.2 ± 0.43
ACORN FEEDERS		
Blue jay	126	1.9 ± 0.76
FRUGIVORES		
Northern flicker (in part)	98	0.7 ± 0.21
GROUND-FEEDING SEED EATERS		
American crow	109	1.0 ± 0.34
Dark-eyed junco	136	0.9 ± 0.39

[a]Excluded are species seen in fewer than 50 percent of the years on January transects.

[b]Listed in descending order of abundance.

oak is reflected in the red-headed woodpecker's being present for less than half of the years, and the only more regular member of the acorn-feeding guild, the blue jay, is more variable from year to year than it is in the gallery forest. Of the gallery forest core group of bark gleaners, only the chickadee and nuthatch are regular in the attenuated forest, and both species have a higher coefficient of variation than that of winter in the gallery forest. In short, life during winter in the attenuated gallery forest is difficult.

In Praise of Standing Dead

The first spring after the Geary County part of Konza Prairie was acquired in 1971 from Mrs. Alf Landon, the various burning treatments were initiated on different watersheds. Three years later Professor Ken Able of SUNY–Albany came to Kansas State University to give a seminar on his studies on migration. The following morning we went out to visit the prairie-chicken lek in 10A, which was then on the McKnight ranch, just to the north. On the way back to the south entrance, Ken called my attention to the song of a Henslow's sparrow. That was the first record for Konza Prairie. We located the bird singing in an unburned watershed, a habitat that eventually would be recognized as almost obligatory for its presence. I was sure that I had not overlooked the species during the previous two breeding seasons, since I was familiar with the bird from my years in Michigan. Although some tracts were not burned the first season, why had it taken three years for the bird to find Konza Prairie? Or, alternatively, why had it taken three years for the habitat to develop acceptable suitability? In any case, the species has occurred on Konza ever since—some years abundantly, some years only uncommonly.

We subsequently discovered that Henslow's sparrows do not usually set up territories in annually burned watersheds but that they can be abundant in watersheds that are burned as frequently as every other year. So if they can use a watershed in the year when it is not torched in April even though burned the year before, the initial absence of Henslow's sparrows on Konza Prairie apparently was not the result of needing three years to attain a level of sufficient suitability; the second year after a fire would have sufficed. It must have been simply that it took that long for the species to find Konza Prairie, since they are uncommon in the region. We have observed also that the same individuals do not come back to Konza Prairie in the following year; they are not philopatric. So their eventually finding Konza Prairie was an expected outcome of their behavioral repertoire. But it took awhile.

Yet not all of the Landon land (or the McKnight ranch for that matter) had been burned every year. Why weren't Henslow's sparrows there from the beginning? It was demonstrated that sufficiently dense standing dead vegetation is an important criterion used in this species' habitat selection. Fire removes standing dead material, but moderate grazing also removes enough live grass so that the amount of standing dead vegetation the following year is insufficient for the needs of the species. It is only in unburned and at most lightly grazed patches of prairie that the species can be regularly found during the breeding season. I'm not sure why this aspect of the habitat is important; perhaps it is the inhibitory effect of standing dead material on live grass stem density, making the ground under the canopy more open for this largely terrestrial bird. I do know, however, that males position their territories to include a greater proportion of this seemingly worthless stuff.

Jerry Wilson joined the Konza Prairie staff after completing a master's degree at Fort Hays State University, having worked on lark buntings. Being interested in birds, he thought it would be worthwhile to set up some bluebird boxes in appropriate habitat along the edge of the gallery forest. He did so, but his boxes never attracted any bluebirds. There are many bluebirds on Konza Prairie, and years later when a bluebird trail was established adjacent to upland prairie along the eastern boundary, bluebirds did come. The trouble was that there also were many natural cavities and old woodpecker holes in standing dead snags. The bluebirds apparently preferred these sites over Jerry's boxes. Bluebirds also will be present in upland prairie if suitable cavities are provided by the presence of standing dead trees. But if natural cavities are lacking, they will readily respond to our offering of nest boxes.

St. Augustine divided nature into three categories: that which was good for man, that which was bad for man, and that which was superfluous to man's well-being. This view of nature was quite reasonable; it reflected the common perception of western people regarding their relationship to the environment. Yet in many ways that perception has often worked to the detriment of nature and even to a decreased probability for humankind's continued existence on the planet. In any case, the notion that grass was only good if it was mowed for hay, grazed by cattle, or intensively managed through annual burning preempted the occurrence of Henslow's sparrows. The notion that dead snags in the forest or in the prairie should either be cut down for firewood or at least removed for safety's sake preempted the nesting of bluebirds (not to mention chickadees, titmouses, and white-footed mice).

It seems people are compelled to manage. That is indeed as it should be, since only humans among all of creation can determine the future trajectory of factors affecting their present situation, predict the consequences of the interactions among these factors, and choose the most efficacious course of future action from among the suite of possible alternatives. That's the value of experience; that's why we invest in a liberal education that compels political science majors to take biology and engineers to take courses in history. The problem arises, however, from an Augustinian, or myopic, view of the world—that is, a view of the world that measures all value in terms of its short-term and most obvious relationship to the immediate well-being of the human condition rather than a far-sighted, holistic view that sees possible choices in the context of the way the entirety of the earth and its biosphere actually works.

We inflict suffering upon ourselves when we let our purposes interfere with the way the world works. Our view is subverted by our egos; we just don't want to see through the eyes of our neighbor, including the biota with which we share this planet. Often our view is truncated by ignorance; we just can't see very far through the haze of uncertainty. And often we decide that the extended consequences of our actions have less value than the immediate rewards. We are impatient. But the important lesson to be learned, I think, is that what we do does make a difference in the future of the biosphere and that this is the arena in which our decisions must be made. We need to correct our myopia by broadening our vision. We must learn to see that there is value in what appears to be superfluous. There is value in standing dead.

4 The Rock Outcrop Shrub Community

Under the shallow Permian seas the continual drizzle of plant and animal remains contributed to the sediments that now form the interbedded layers of limestone and shales that give the Flint Hills Upland its terraced profile. As these sedimentary rocks were uplifted, they tilted slightly toward the west (Jewett 1941). This dip of just a few degrees from the horizontal led to a series of events that resulted in the development of the rock outcrop shrub community and its small but largely unique assemblage of birds (Table 1).

Rain and snow melt either run off across the surface of the soil, eventually finding their way into the rivulets and channels in the upper reaches of the watersheds that form dendritic patterns across the landscape of Konza Prairie, or this water seeps into the soil. Here it might be bound to clays, might return to the atmosphere again by evaporation, or might continue down— moving slowly through the shales but more rapidly through the cracks and crevices of the fractured limestone strata, following the pull of gravity, and emerging on the surface where these limestone formations outcrop as distinct benches (Fig. 20). Thus along these ledges, especially in association with the Cottonwood, Eiss, and Crouse limestones but as high as the Threemile limestones of the Wreford Formation (Fig. 21), flowing water appears as seeps and springs, either along the broad front of the outcrop or at the head of a small valley, that provide sufficient moisture to support woody vegetation. In a series of transects over a distance of 1,021 m through this habitat, 70 percent of the

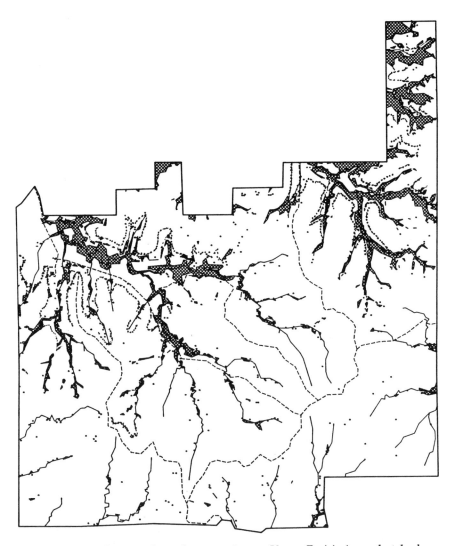

Figure 20. Distribution of woody vegetation on Konza Prairie (cross-hatched areas). Forested habitats extend from the gallery forest in the valleys of Kings and Shane creeks to the attenuated gallery forest at higher elevations in these stream drainages. The rock outcrop shrub community (rows of dots) is best expressed along the Cottonwood and Eiss limestones but also develops above these benches along the Crouse and Threemile limestones. Individual dots or groups of dots indicate isolated woody patches. Dashed lines are major Jeep trails.

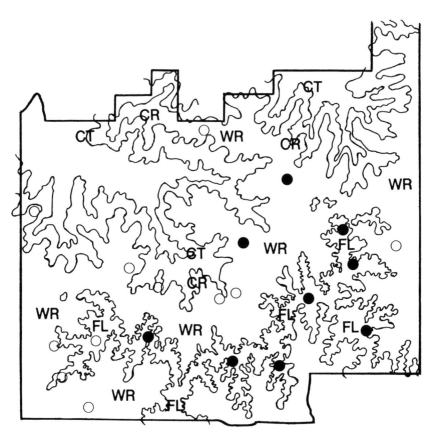

Figure 21. Locations of primary (solid circles) and satellite (open circles) greater prairie-chicken leks on Konza Prairie. Also indicated are the Florence limestone (FL) on the highest elevations in the southern half of Konza Prairie, upon which most of the primary leks are located; the broad, sloping apron overlying the Wreford limestone (WR) formation, on which the remaining leks are located; and the major benches formed from the Crouse (CR) and Cotton-wood (CT) limestones. The Eiss limestone forms a bench between these two outcrops and the Threemile limestone outcrops in the lower Wreford.

cover was provided by rough-leaved dogwood, 9 percent by aromatic sumac, 7 percent by American elm, and 6 percent by plum. Of the remaining cover, 5 percent was variously composed of red cedar, redbud, chinquapin oak, honey locust, hackberry, prickly ash, and smooth sumac. Only 3 percent was open.

Bewick's wrens are restricted in their nesting habitat to the attenuated gallery forest, where they find natural cavities. They will, however, use artificial nesting sites.

Eastern kingbirds breed in tallgrass prairie and migrate through the region in large numbers during late summer.

Upland sandpipers forage in burned prairie but usually nest in unburned prairie.

The eastern meadowlark's sturdy bill allows it to probe through the tangle of litter and growing grass stems to secure insects.

Numbers of lark sparrows will probably increase as grazing by bison results in more open ground cover.

The dickcissel is the most abundant territorial species on Konza Prairie.

Perennially present during the summer in the gallery forest, the red-headed woodpecker winters elsewhere when bur oak acorns are scarce.

American tree sparrow is the most regular and most abundant species during the winter in the grassland community.

Arriving in early May from the neotropics, yellow-billed cuckoos are prominent insectivores in gallery forest but also occur in unburned prairie.

The black-capped chickadee resides in forested habitats during both winter and summer.

The broad diet of the red-bellied woodpecker results in stable populations through the years.

Male Henslow's sparrows select territories with higher densities of standing dead vegetation, but they will use song perches in woody vegetation.

Brown-headed cowbirds lay their eggs in the nests of host species breeding in all Konza bird communities.

The continued presence of greater prairie-chickens is indicative of well-managed tallgrass prairie.

Common nighthawks nest in both burned and unburned grassland but roosting flocks occur within the gallery forest during migration.

A recently fledged common poorwill sits on the rock that served as its nest site.

While more common in forested habitats, downy woodpeckers search shrubs and stouter forbs for food in grassland sites.

Grasshopper sparrows are equally abundant in burned and unburned grassland.

White-breasted nuthatch is a common permanent resident in the gallery and attenuated forests.

To move from the two-dimensional horizon of the prairie into the closed, three-dimensional space of these 2- to 3-m tall woody thickets requires an adjustment in perspective. The growth forms of the plants are various. Dogwood confines its foliage to the extremity of the branches, resulting in an open thicket of minimally branched living and dead stems under the canopy. The thicker trunks of elms jut upward within the thickets, as do the more-difficult-to-penetrate branching patterns of aromatic sumac, prickly ash that rips, and plum that jabs with its short, stout side branches. The average density of woody stems in these patches is high, ranging from 9 to 11 stems/m^2 (Farley 1987).

The occurrences of Bell's vireos on June transects in unburned grassland (Fig. 11) result from the presence of rock outcrop shrubs within the watershed, since the delicate branching of the dogwoods provides the suitable forks from which this vireo suspends its slightly pendulant nest. All may be quiet when you enter a thicket belonging to a Bell's vireo, but a few simulated alarm notes ("pishes") will immediately bring the male scolding to inquire of the nature of your intrusion, coming to within a meter or so of your face while you sit quietly within the cavern of the vegetation. Often the female will join in the defense of thicket ownership.

The nests are easy to find; they are usually placed in the open under the dogwood canopy, about 1 m off the ground, and built in an area of the thicket where the density of dead stems is low (Farley 1987). They are also easily found by predators and especially the parasitic brown-headed cowbird, both of which are important causes for nest failure. Only 35 percent of the breeding adults fledge at least one offspring because of the combined effects of parasitism and predation. In Greg Farley's study (1987) about half (48.6 percent) of the nests were abandoned because of cowbird parasitism: If one or more cowbird eggs were laid prior to the laying of the third vireo egg, the female vireo would desert (see also Barlow 1962).

79

Another characteristic bird of the rock outcrop shrubs is the black-billed cuckoo. Its presence remains covert for most of the season. Only in late spring and early summer, when the male offers his segmented, syncopated series of "cuh-cuh's," is one aware of the bird. It is seldom recorded on June transects in unburned grassland and infrequently on attenuated gallery forest censuses where it is a member of the shrub patch habitat that interfaces with grasslands (Fig. 18). But on the horizontal branches in these shrub thickets the female builds a stick nest and lays her two or three eggs. The female sits tightly, being reluctant to flush; if you move quietly through the interior of the thicket, she slips off the nest silently only when you reach out from within fingertip distance of her nest. Black-billed cuckoos are probably more abundant than we suspect, but because of their reclusive behavior we overlook them; they are quite different from the yellow-billed cuckoo that persistently sings from the attenuated gallery forest lower down in the watersheds as well as in the gallery forest.

All three of the mimics—brown thrasher, gray catbird, and northern mockingbird—occur in the rock outcrop community. Brown thrashers, however, are not unique to this habitat, since they often choose nest sites in isolated elms or small thickets within unburned grassland as well as establishing territories in forest habitats. But along shrubby rock outcrops each thick elm that thrusts up through the canopy of the dominant dogwoods should be searched for the nest of the thrasher, whose behavior is the complete opposite of that of the cuckoo. The thrasher chooses an exposed perch above the thicket, often in the same elm harboring the nest, to sing and sing in paired phrases from the end of April to the end of August and can still be found lurking in the thickets, giving scolding calls, until mid-October. The gray catbird only occurs in the rock outcrop shrub community. This species, however, is less common than the thrasher, and its numbers fluctuate from year to year. Northern mockingbirds are even more infrequent, occurring most readily in thickets adjacent to grassland overgrazed by cattle—for example, lower Texas Hog pasture.

The Bewick's wren forages in the outcrop shrub community but prefers nesting habitats with lower stem densities and higher tree canopies (Farley 1987)—that is, in the attenuated gallery forest. Nests of Bewick's wrens are located within the cavities of trees; nests placed in short snags or near the tops of taller snags are the more productive (Farley 1987). About three-fourths of the females on Konza Prairie attempt more than one brood during the nesting season. Dale Kennedy has attracted Bewick's wrens to nest boxes placed along the edge of the gallery forest in lower Shane Creek. For the moment it is not known if this will result in the invasion of the gallery forest by Bewick's wrens, where they perhaps will come into direct competition with Carolina wrens or house wrens, or whether the yearlings produced in the boxes will establish their territories higher in the watershed.

Some species that occur in the rock outcrop shrub community during the summer are more characteristic of other habitats (northern cardinal, field sparrow, American goldfinch). The fruits displayed by dogwood in August are perhaps critical to the migratory flocks of kingbirds. Reduction of dogwood patches by persistent annual burning would probably have a major negative impact on the portion of this population that migrates southward through the Flint Hills. This habitat also attracts wandering species in late summer (white-eyed vireo) as well as in winter (mountain bluebird), and these shrubby patches appear to be critical as safe havens for tree sparrows that forage during winter in adjacent grasslands.

Although annual fires will eventually eliminate this localized habitat, rock outcrop shrubs persist under all other burning treatments and certainly formed a characteristic patch community in the primeval prairie. Its presence has led to colonization by a small suite of species that invaded the prairie from farther east and as a result increased the diversity in the assemblage that is characteristic of the tallgrass prairie.

81

5   Prairie-chickens

Dawn is still an hour away, just a faint prelude on the eastern horizon, on the spring mornings every year when many hardy folks follow the trail from the south entrance of Konza Prairie to the prairie-chicken blind that has been established in 10A for use by the public. The blind is available from early March to mid-May, although the reservations list is close to capacity by Thanksgiving. Even though the male chickens begin to get serious in February about their annual attempt to win the favored copulation, from late March to mid-April is the best time to visit because females start coming to the lek during the last week of March to choose this season's mate. Mating reaches a peak in the first week of April, yet females still come in May. Robel (1970) showed that nests initiated after the first of May have a significantly lowered chance of success than nests begun earlier, and Bowen (1971) observed a reduction in clutch size as the nesting season progresses. Although time is critical, females are deliberate, visiting one or several leks (Robel et al. 1970) for several days before they mate (Robel and Ballard 1974). But then they do not come back, unless they must renest. And nest loss occurs regularly on Konza Prairie because of April burning schedules.

On calm mornings the walk to the blind is accompanied by gentle songs of recently arrived poorwills calling from along the rock outcrops, bidding good day to the dwindling darkness. If you have timed your journey well, you are in the blind before the male prairie-chickens arrive and need only wait half an hour or so in the dark while the cold seeps into your bones. It is usually windy at the booming ground, since leks are typically established on exposed ridges where there is greater visibility and audibility. Furthermore, the shallow claypan soils characteristic of these sites are covered by arid-adapted grama grasses that provide shorter and sparser vegetation, offering little impediment to the display of the males (Horak 1985). The thin plywood walls of the blind pulse with the gusts, and the guy wires sing—but the birds will come.

While still too dark for birders to see well, an eastern meadowlark proclaims his territory, having already attracted a mate who is incubating a nest containing four speckled eggs and probably a cowbird egg as well. Although waiting expectantly, you are still surprised to hear the first "old-mul-doon" of a male chicken that had walked unnoticed onto the booming ground in the dim gray of the predawn. Soon you see others flying to the periphery and then walking onto the grounds while some fly directly to their position in the well-defined territorial matrix of the lek. Individual territories are not large, averaging from 86 to 518 m² (Horak 1985; Robel 1964, 1965; Ballard and Robel 1974). Watching individually marked birds, Robel (1964, 1965) was able to discern three regions within each male's territory: an innermost *sanctum sanctorum* that no other male ever entered and that made up about 13 percent of the total territory, a middle secondary region into which neighboring males occasionally intruded, and a peripheral region where almost all aggressive encounters with contiguous males occurred.

These confrontations are highly stereotyped. Syringeal cackles are interspersed between the booming sounds reverberating from the birds' cervical air sacs, a concerto grosso pattern accentuated with struts and bows that merges with that of neighboring birds to produce an intensity of sound that can be heard from about two km away. Seldom do the birds make physical contact, but intense displays do involve birds jumping up together and flapping breast to breast. Females walk on, almost

83

nonchalantly, seemingly unmoved by the frantic activity all around them. After a short while in the blind you begin to decipher the language—the sequence of treading, bowing, and booming; the crouched posture and the depressed pinnae of the loser in a male-to-male confrontation; the increased cacophony of cackles when a female approaches; the subtle invitational display of the female that leads to copulation—so that you can soon read the drama, a play that has unfolded every morning of every spring for thousands and thousands of years. But this play's final curtain descends when well-managed prairie is either degraded by overgrazing or converted into other uses.

At this particular lek the dominant bird always has the territory by the old buffalo wallow. The bird is not always the same each year, since older individuals are in time replaced by new males. What is it about this particular territory that makes it so preferred? The rewards are certainly great, since this male does most of the mating, and along with the next-most-dominant male accounts for approximately 85 percent of all the copulations (Robel 1964). Robel and Ballard (1974) showed that the presence of the two most dominant males influences the maintenance of the territorial pattern. When the researchers removed the dominant birds during the lekking season, the remaining males spent so much time and energy jockeying for the now vacated dominant positions that the rate of successful copulation on the lek was drastically reduced.

Sometimes the display is abruptly truncated by a predator. Coyotes often pass by, but if they do not get close to the lek the male prairie-chickens usually just hunker down and remain quiet rather than flushing. This response to a ground predator, however, has had grave consequences. Once observers in the blind had the rare experience of seeing a bobcat capture a male chicken and carry it off to a dogwood thicket below the adjacent ridge, where the predator was found later leisurely devouring its prey. The passage of avian predators usually elicits flight by the entire lek. But escape is not always successful—another group of birders was fortunate enough to see a migrant prairie falcon successfully take a bird from the lek. Northern harriers are the usual cause of the birds' flushing, even though the hawk's crossing is inadvertent as it searches for rodents. But harriers do occasionally make a pass at the birds; perhaps it is just for fun, although Haukos and Broda (1989) found them to prey on lesser prairie-chickens (*Tympanuchus pallidicinctus*).

About two hours after dawn, activity begins to wane. The rate of display decreases markedly, males often sitting quietly in their territories or walking about grazing or at least simulating grazing by pecking in the sparse vegetation. The sun is well above the horizon now, and the other sounds of the prairie replace the now muted noise of the lek—small, chattering flocks of brown-headed cowbirds flying close to the ground in pursuit of single females pass across your view, an upland sandpiper's "wolf-whistle" punctuates its parabolic flight rising above the next ridge, the buzzing trill of a grasshopper sparrow erupts from close at hand. Meadowlarks forage between the quiescent cocks, and sometimes a relatively uncommon horned lark finds the short grass of the booming ground suitable for a brief search for insects as it interrupts its flight across Konza from the greening wheat fields and more heavily grazed pastures where it finds nesting habitat more to its liking. When you leave the blind the birds will flush, but some birds will return again that morning. Almost all of them will reassemble in the evening, but the display then is more subdued.

Twenty different leks have been identified on Konza Prairie since surveys began in 1981 (Table 13), although no more than 13 have been active in any given year (Fig. 22). Of these, five have persisted through all the years (although no survey was taken in 1990), and nine (45 percent) have been present at least 80 percent of the years. Seven of these primary leks are situated on the highest ridges of Florence limestone; the other two are on the broader, yet still exposed aprons underlain by the Wreford limestone formation (Fig. 21). This topographic association of the

85

TABLE 13 Mean Size of Numbers of Birds per Year, Coefficient of
Variation, and Frequency of Use for Each of the Twenty
Prairie-Chicken Leks on Konza Prairie, 1981–1991

Mean Size[a]	Coefficient of Variation	Frequency of Use (%)[b]
25.7 ± 2.70	33.2	100
8.7 ± 1.08	39.4	100
13.1 ± 1.45	33.2	90
19.9 ± 3.10	44.0	80
14.0 ± 0	—	10
11.6 ± 1.78	48.6	100
9.0 ± 0	—	10
12.0 ± 6.00	70.1	20
10.0 ± 5.00	70.7	20
2.5 ± 0.50	28.3	20
14.3 ± 1.35	29.8	100
14.0 ± 1.48	33.5	100
7.6 ± 1.84	68.4	80
15.0 ± 6.35	73.3	30
10.0 ± 0	—	10
5.5 ± 3.53	90.1	20
3.0 ± 0	0.0	20
14.0 ± 3.14	63.4	80
6.0 ± 0	0.0	20
5.0 ± 1.00	28.3	20

— = no variation (one year's data only).
[a] ± S.E.
[b]No data for 1990

leks is characteristic for the species. The other 11 leks appear
ephemeral, being present for one year or intermittently for two or
three years and then being discontinued. All but two of these have
been located below the highest ridges. No leks fall into a frequency
of occupancy between 30 and 80 percent. Whatever factors determine the selection of a site by a group of chickens, tenacity to a specific site appears to be determined from the experiences over just a
couple of seasons. Or alternatively, during the period of these observations chicken populations only reached a level that resulted in
heavy use of the secondary or satellite leks in four of the years (see

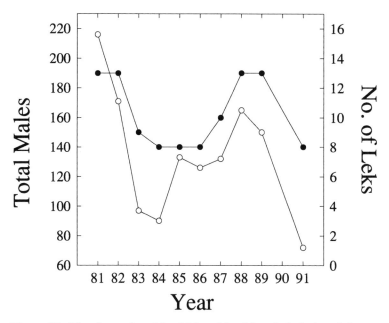

Figure 22. Numbers of prairie-chicken leks (closed circles) and the total number of males recorded at all leks (open circles) during spring surveys from 1981 through 1991.

the following discussion). If populations had been continually high, perhaps satellite leks would have been more frequently used—indeed, have become primary leks.

The population of males on each of the booming grounds is relatively constant throughout a single season. Most of the variation occurs before mid-April and is largely due to movements of nonterritorial adults and younger males between leks (Robel et al. 1970). Year-to-year variation is largely the result of changes in numbers of "incidental males" (Horak 1985). The size of the lek may also be a factor affecting stability through the years. When this hypothesis is tested by correlating mean lek size with the coefficients of variation for the means of the number of territorial males of each of the nine leks that have been used for at least 80 percent of the years (Table 13), there is a significant inverse relationship (Spearman $r = -0.60$, $N = 9$, $P < 0.05$). When the mean

87

of the average lek sizes of these nine leks ($\bar{x} = 23.4$) is compared to that of those leks existing for 30 percent of the years or less ($\bar{x} = 8.4$), the difference is also significant (Student's $t = 6.85$, $df = 18$, $P < 0.01$). Larger leks are more stable. Schroeder and Braun (1992) also have recently demonstrated this relationship.

Horak (1985) suggested that when total prairie-chicken populations are high, competition is intense, and nonterritorial birds are thwarted in their attempts to enter existing leks. In response, they set up small, satellite booming grounds. If the total male population each year for all leks on Konza Prairie (Fig. 22) is correlated with the number of leks present that year that are short-lived, the hypothesis that the number of satellite leks is directly related to the total male population is supported (Pearson $r = 0.74$, $N = 10$, $P < 0.02$).

The prairie-chicken, or prairie grouse as it is sometimes called, is appropriately named. The numbers of dickcissels might be affected by factors on the wintering grounds, no matter what the condition of the prairie might be. Furthermore, the prairie is only the dickcissel's secondary choice. The occurrence of Henslow's sparrows is sporadic, being dependent upon the availability of standing dead vegetation in unburned grasslands, but this species can utilize a broad spectrum of grasslands, including successional meadows. Grasshopper sparrows and eastern meadowlarks are readily found in tame brome pastures or other tracts devoted to agricultural activities. Even upland sandpipers have adapted to human modification of prairie habitats. The greater prairie-chicken, however, is the bellwether of the tallgrass prairie. As long as these birds' overture to the rising sun can be consistently heard upon an April morning, you can be assured that the true prairie remains alive and well, at least in that locale.

Migration

Bird watchers enjoy their hobby because it allows them to experience environments that are normally not characteristic of the workplace, whether that be home, the shop, or even outside. Time "in the field" restores the spirit. It is indeed recreational, even in unpleasant weather. Birders gain satisfaction from meeting the challenge of being able to name a bird, often on the basis of difficult-to-discern criteria, and there is always the chance that they will see a species they have never seen before or one that is completely out of place, either temporally or geographically or both. There are also those birders who just like to make lists. All these folks look forward to the seasons of passage, when both variety and numbers of birds reach their peaks as populations move through on their migratory journeys between breeding and wintering ranges.

Almost half of all the species observed at Konza Prairie are migrants; they spend neither summer nor winter there. They, like the people driving the interstate highway along the south border of Konza Prairie, are transients—just passin' through. The wedges and staggered echelons of Canada, white-fronted, and snow geese and the stacked planes of spirally soaring white pelicans form patterns across the vault of the sky that make the impact of migration on the prairie different from that in the East where there is no horizon. But these species never stop and thus do not contribute to the list of Konza birds. Some waterfowl do alight when the habitat is suitable. Thus in those years when the ponds have water in spring there are coots and waders, puddle ducks like teal and gadwall, and divers like ring-necks. Snipe and rails flush from marshy swales. But in the fall when the bottoms of the ponds are frequently layered with dust and the beds of the streams that form the limestone-gray backbones of watersheds are exposed and swept clean by the wind that rattles the browned stalks of cattails, there are no water birds at all.

Many migrants are quite selective in their choices of habitat even though their residency on Konza Prairie is transitory. Spring burning removes litter and standing dead material, modifying the habitat and increasing the accessibility of food for a variety of ground-feeding species. Blackened watersheds are visited by Franklin's gulls, American pipits, and Brewer's blackbirds, species that seldom stop on Konza Prairie during their autumnal passage. The lesser golden-plovers on their spring rush through the Great Plains are only observed in association with these burns. In both spring and fall vesper sparrows concentrate along fireguards and Jeep trails, selecting mowed grass in preference to the deeper thatch of the prairie. Similarly this is the singular habitat patch in which longspurs and Sprague's pipits are found. Although the olive-sided flycatchers are broad generalists in their occurrence from the lower gallery forest to the upper terminus of the attenuated gallery forest, they are quite narrow in their selection of dead snags that rise above the tree canopy from which to make their foraging sallies. In contrast, the more common transients are ubiquitous in their habitat choice. Species like least flycatchers, ruby-crowned kinglets, yellow-rumped and orange-crowned warblers, Lincoln's and white-crowned sparrows drop out of the sky to forage in all habitats.

When I was younger I preferred spring migration. Maybe that is because I was in Ohio and Michigan, where the brilliant, nuptial-clad wood warblers dominate the vernal aspect and the songs of the woodland thrushes invite your entry into stands of beech and maple. Now I prefer the fall migration. I really don't think it is a function of the advent of my own autumn, rather it is biogeographical. The prairie is different. Spring warbler migration in the prairie is almost exclusively yellow-rumps and orange-crowns; only occasionally is there the flash of a black-throated green or a Blackburnian. And it is quiet. Transients like northern waterthrushes (*Seiurus noveboracensis*) that sing to establish territories during their migratory stopovers are rare. And even though Swainson's thrushes are sometimes common and do sing during their passage through the gallery forest, the rest of the woodwind section in the dawn chorus of the eastern forests is missing.

Frontal passage in fall is calm in contrast to the usual turbulence of spring, and in its wake the forests and rock outcrop shrubs are full of sparrows washed down with the gentle rain—swamp sparrows, white-throats, and fox sparrows from the northern woods, Harris' sparrows from the edge of the taiga, and spotted (rufous-sided) towhees down from the mountains. In the prairie cordgrass along upland watersheds, numerous Le Conte's sparrows decorate the tops of the grasses with their ochre faces. And they linger for days, whereas in spring they hurry through so fast that they are seldom seen. After spending the previous evening feeding on acorns, hundreds of blue jays depart in the early morning from roosts in the attenuated gallery forest and move southward in long narrow columns, up the valley and then over the ridge, flying low across the prairie. Flocks of robins pass through the gallery forest like swirls of blowing leaves, sometimes pausing for days to deplete an abundant hackberry crop. Mississippi kites wander into the Flint Hills during fall, and merlins spend some time hunting along the edge of the forest.

Maybe I prefer the fall migration simply because it is the last hurrah of the year, a sharp contrast with winter that begins to settle down across Konza Prairie by late November. Winter is not especially harsh, but the upland prairie is often devoid of any birds. When traversing January transects, the only sound is that of my boots parting the dry, siliceous grasses. In the gallery forest, only a few mixed-species flocks of bark-gleaning insectivores move through the quiet void. Even in years when the bur oak acorns are abundant and the red-headed woodpeckers remain, diversity is still slim even though the woods are a little noisier. By late February the waterfowl are moving overhead, but Konza Prairie below remains still in its winter doldrums. It is not until March—when a Bewick's wren first decides to sing, when wintering bluebirds are first joined by birds from farther south, and when the first field sparrows appear as the vanguard of passerine migration—that spring is announced, and the birds' prairie year begins anew.

6 Annotated List of the Birds of Konza Prairie

Species accounts cover the period 1971 through 1992; unless otherwise noted, they are based on my observations. During the first 10 years of this period, records are more infrequent and largely limited to the breeding season. With the initiation of the LTER program on Konza Prairie in 1981, visits were made at least once a week throughout every year. Visits were made almost daily during the breeding seasons in the early 1980s in order to develop a more comprehensive nesting record. American white pelicans, three species of geese, and many other waterfowl, as well as shorebirds, fly over Konza Prairie during their migratory journeys, but they are not included in this list. Species that are included were found on the ground or, if in flight, were searching for food over the Konza terrain (for example, swallows and raptors).

The majority of records of waterfowl, shorebirds, rails, and other water-dependent species occur during the spring. By late summer and autumn the appropriate habitat has often evaporated. Some common species that should have been seen—for example, northern shoveler—have not been discovered, and of course many uncommon and rare transients have been missed. Yet this annotated list provides the best accounting currently available of the avifauna of the Flint Hills.

Nesting data are available in LTER data set CBN01 and dates of record in LTER data set CBD01. These files are open and continue to be used as a repository for records. Visitors to Konza

Prairie should contact the LTER data manager to contribute documented sightings of species and confirmed breeding activity.

Pied-billed Grebe, *Podilymbus podiceps* (Linnaeus)

This occasional migrant stops briefly in spring and fall on the deeper stock ponds, for example, Southgate, Thirteen, and White Pasture ponds. Inclusive dates are 20 March to 22 April and 21 September to 29 October.

Double-crested Cormorant, *Phalacrocorax auritus* (Lesson)

Although cormorants are regularly seen flying over Konza Prairie during both spring and autumnal periods of passage, the only two recorded instances of cormorants alighting on any ponds occurred on 9 and 16 October 1990, when Jennifer Harris found two birds on Thirteen Pond.

American Bittern, *Botaurus lentiginosus* (Rackett)

There are only two records for this rare spring migrant. On 19 April 1982, during burning, Elmer Finck observed one flushed from a cattail stand along upper Pressee Branch, and he discovered another on the east fork of Swede Creek on 2 April 1983.

Great Blue Heron, *Ardea herodias* Linnaeus

During spring and summer, great blues fly over the prairie between a nesting colony on Deep Creek east of Konza Prairie and feeding sites along the Kansas River. This species is also an uncommon visitor along lower Kings Creek and several stock ponds, with sightings almost weekly from 1 March until late September. During October the great blue heron is an occasional visitor if there is sufficient water along Kings Creek, but there are only two records for November. There are a few records from 5 to 29 December but only a single January record (5 January 1984). If Kings Creek or spring-fed ponds remain open, herons can increasingly be found during February.

Great Egret, *Casmerodius albus* (Linnaeus)

A single bird was discovered on 6 April 1982 at the stock pond in N20A.

Cattle Egret, *Bubulcus ibis* (Linnaeus)

At the present time this heron is a rare spring visitor. Lloyd Hulbert reported a single bird in May 1978, associated with cattle when they were pastured in the brome field along the north fork of Kings Creek. On 4 May 1986, John Briggs saw one in the wheat field along the entrance road to the headquarters area.

Green-backed Heron, *Butorides striatus* (Linnaeus)

The green-backed heron, an uncommon summer resident, is consistently seen from mid-April to mid-September along the upper drainages as well as on the main stem of Kings Creek. The earliest date is 21 April, and the latest date is 25 September. Elmer Finck found a nest on 4 June 1983 with three eggs about 1 m above the water in a willow standing in about 0.3 m of water at the upper end of Southgate Pond, but this nest was empty on 13 June. Other pairs of green-backed herons are regularly seen along lower Kings Creek during summer, but no nests have been discovered.

Black-crowned Night-heron, *Nycticorax nycticorax* (Linnaeus)

The only record of the black-crowned night-heron for Konza Prairie is a juvenile bird observed along an unforested portion of lower Kings Creek on 17 September 1985.

Yellow-crowned Night-heron, *Nyctanassa violaceus* (Linnaeus)

The single record for this species is a juvenile bird observed on 3 September 1991 along the reach of Kings Creek where the black-crowned night-heron had been observed.

95

Wood Duck, *Aix sponsa* (Linnaeus)

This uncommon summer resident occurs in the gallery forest along Kings Creek; it arrives in early March (9 March) but is more difficult to find after the first week in June. Mark Heinrich saw a female wood duck entering a presumed nesting hole 6 m up in a bur oak on 31 May 1983 along the south fork of Kings Creek. A female with a brood was seen on the south fork of Kings Creek on 15 July 1981. There are two fall records—1 October 1984 and 31 October 1984—and Sharon Gurtz saw a bird on Kings Creek by the Hokansen house on 10 January 1987.

Green-winged Teal, *Anas crecca* Linnaeus

This duck is an occasional migrant, most regular on Southgate Pond during March (as early as 4 March) and early April (10 April). One fall record occurred on 10 November 1984 on the pond in N20A.

Mallard, *Anas platyrhynchos* Linnaeus

Mallards occur in fall from 12 October to 30 November and pass through in spring until 20 April; they are found on stock ponds and Kings Creek. The species also is present during winter months, being especially regular as a winter resident along lower Kings Creek when the Kansas River becomes largely ice covered.

Blue-winged Teal, *Anas discors* Linnaeus

This species is an occasional spring migrant on stock ponds, particularly Southgate and N20A ponds, with dates ranging from 18 March to 4 May. There are no fall records, because ponds are often dry.

Gadwall, *Anas strepera* Linnaeus

A few records have been obtained during migration (13 March 1984, 31 October 1984), but primarily the gadwall is an uncommon winter resident along lower Kings Creek and on open stock ponds. Like the mallard, it is most regular along lower Kings Creek, sometimes in relatively large flocks (e.g., 18 birds on 27 December 1983).

American Wigeon, *Anas americana* Gmelin

The only records for the American wigeon are for the White Pasture Pond during spring migration in 1988, when 11 birds were present on 9 March and two birds were still there on 21 March.

Ring-necked Duck, *Aythya collaris* (Donovan)

The expected diving duck on small ponds, this uncommon migrant has been recorded only in the spring from 28 February until 20 April, with most dates of presence throughout March. The ring-necked duck occurs on various stock ponds: for example, Thirteen, Texas Hog, and especially Southgate, where 14 birds were present on 30 March 1984.

Common Goldeneye, *Bucephala clangula* (Linnaeus)

The goldeneye is an occasional winter visitor, occurring on lower Kings Creek (two males on 19 February 1986) or on open stock ponds (Thirteen, 28 November 1984).

Bufflehead, *Bucephala albeola* (Linnaeus)

This species is an occasional visitor to Southgate Pond, recorded during migration (27 March 1985) and in winter (18 December 1971).

Hooded Merganser, *Lophodytes cucullatus* (Linnaeus)

This species is an occasional migrant. A female was present on White Pasture Pond on 15 April 1983 and another female on Southgate Pond on 19 November 1985.

97

Ruddy Duck, *Oxyura jamaicensis* (Gmelin)

The only record of a ruddy duck is a female found freshly dead in the headquarters area by Joe Gelroth on 27 October 1983.

Turkey Vulture, *Cathartes aura* (Linnaeus)

The vulture is an uncommon summer visitor, occurring from mid-March (18 March) to early October (7 October). It is most common during migration in late March and April. Latest date is 19 October.

Osprey, *Pandion haliaetus* (Linnaeus)

This bird is an uncommon migrant in the region, especially in fall, but there are only three records for Konza Prairie—two fall records (8 September 1982 and 18 September 1984) and a winter record on 6 January 1982.

Mississippi Kite, *Ictinia mississippiensis* (Wilson)

Konza Prairie is on the eastern fringe of this species' range; it is an occasional transient during September along the gallery forest edge and the attenuated gallery forest. There are two summer records: a bird seen by Neil Schanker on 7 June 1987 and another seen by Elmer Finck on 8 July 1982.

Bald Eagle, *Haliaeetus leucocephalus* (Linnaeus)

Although a common winter resident along the Kansas River, this raptor is occasionally seen on Konza Prairie soaring over the ridge along the north boundary and sometimes perched on the taller trees on lower Kings Creek near the entrance road. Dates span the period from 21 November to 27 February.

Northern Harrier, *Circus cyaneus* (Linnaeus)

Records for this species occur in almost every week of the year. The northern harrier is an uncommon summer resident in both unburned and burned grasslands during March through early July but is less frequently seen during the last three weeks in

July. It becomes uncommon again in late August and then common from October through December, with numbers tapering off during January and February. Numbers of wintering birds are dependent upon the density of prey species, particularly cotton rats (*Sigmodon hispidus*). For example, northern harriers were absent in the winter of 1983–1984 when cotton rat populations were low. There are two nesting records from unburned watersheds: a nest with six eggs along the north fork of Pressee Branch in 1982 that resulted in two fledged young (Finck 1984a) and another discovered by Greg Farley in the center of a buckbrush clump with five eggs on 15 May 1986 in N20A.

Sharp-shinned Hawk, *Accipiter striatus* Vieillot

Sharpies are common during migration along the edge of the gallery forest and in the attenuated gallery forest along both the Kings Creek and Shane Creek drainages. The period of fall passage is from early September (2 September) through late October (31 October), whereas in spring the bird is transient during March and April (4 March to 15 April). The sharp-shinned hawk is an uncommon winter resident from November through February. There is one summer record, a bird seen on 13 July 1986 by Elmer Finck.

Cooper's Hawk, *Accipiter cooperii* (Bonaparte)

This hawk is an occasional winter resident in habitats similar to those used by the sharp-shinned hawk. Transients pass through in October, but the earliest arrival date for winter residents is 30 November. Most observations are during January and February. The latest spring date is 4 May. There is one summer record, 16 June 1983, of a bird soaring over upland grassland (N20B). On 9 March 1990, a juvenile bird was discovered on the main trail adjacent to 20B feeding on a male greater prairie-chicken that it had apparently taken from the lek in this upland prairie site.

99

Northern Goshawk, *Accipiter gentilis* (Linnaeus)

During winter and spring of 1983 an adult male frequented lower Kings Creek from 14 January until 16 April. A second record is of a juvenile seen in late September 1987 by Elmer Finck; I saw the same bird on 1 October in the upper end of the gallery forest along the south fork of Kings Creek. More recently David Rintoul obtained a surprisingly late record on 25 April 1992.

Broad-winged Hawk, *Buteo platypterus* (Vieillot)

There are only two records of this rare spring transient. A single bird was soaring over the gallery forest along the north fork of Kings Creek on 13 April 1984. The other record was also a single bird flying over the prairie east of lower Kings Creek on 19 April 1991.

Swainson's Hawk, *Buteo swainsoni* Bonaparte

Although Swainson's hawks nest on the floodplain of the Kansas River in Riley County, no behavior even suggestive of breeding has been observed on Konza Prairie. This species is an uncommon spring migrant; earliest date is 19 March, but most records have been obtained during April, and the latest date is 18 May. It is an occasional summer visitor (21 June 1972, 26 July 1982) and fall transient from 30 August to 24 October.

Red-tailed Hawk, *Buteo jamaicensis* (Gmelin)

Approximately five pairs of red-tailed hawks breed on Konza Prairie, building nests along the edge of the gallery forest and in more isolated stands in the attenuated gallery forest along tributaries of both Kings and Shane creeks. Nests are usually started in winter, and by late February pairs can be found perched side by side at completed nests. Young are present in the nest by late April (24 April). Birds have used bur oak and sycamore for nest trees. The species is an uncommon permanent resident, having been recorded during every week of the year. Red-tails become more abundant from December through April as a result of the influx of a winter resident population that usually includes melanistic morphs and *B. j. harlani*.

Rough-legged Hawk, *Buteo lagopus* (Pontoppidan)

This uncommon winter resident occurs from late September (27 September) to early April (10 April), when it can be observed hunting above grassland sites. Most records, however, are from November through January. In some years this species is absent (1984) or only occasional (1988).

Golden Eagle, *Aquila chrysaetos* (Linnaeus)

This large and impressive raptor is an occasional winter visitor, arriving as early as 8 October and remaining into March (16 March). In any given year, there is usually only one bird; but in 1990 both an adult and a subadult bird were seen during winter.

American Kestrel, *Falco sparverius* Linneaus

Our smallest falcon is a permanent resident. It is uncommon during summer months (about seven to eight pairs) but becomes common from October through April when transients and wintering birds are present. The American kestrel is often abundant on newly burned watersheds in April, occurring in widely spaced, loose groups of 10 to 12 birds. Most of these are probably migrants, but the groups could include resident birds from Konza and adjacent areas. Nest sites are typically old woodpecker holes in dead snags along the upper reaches of the major stream drainages. Earliest copulation observed was in March (28 March 1983), and fledged young accompanied by an adult have been seen in June (25 June 1982).

Merlin, *Falco columbarius* Linnaeus

This occasional transient occurs in fall and as a winter visitant. There are only four records: 10 January 1981, 26 February 1986, 25 October 1989, and 12 November 1988.

101

Prairie Falcon, *Falco mexicanus* Schlegel

This uncommon transient and winter visitor is present from early September (3 September) until mid-April (16 April). Gary Schiltz saw a prairie falcon attempting to take a prairie-chicken at the lek in 10A on 1 April 1984.

Peregrine Falcon, *Falco peregrinus* Tunstall

Peregrines are occasional spring transients from March (24 March) through early May (2 May). There is only one fall record—a bird seen by Jennifer Harris on 18 September 1990—and no winter records. On 5 April 1985 Elmer Finck discovered a peregrine eating a prairie-chicken on the lek in 20B. Upon Finck's approach, the peregrine flew off with the prairie-chicken in its talons at about 1 m above the ground, disappearing over the edge of a hill about 70 m away. Peregrines harassing prairie-chickens have been observed from the public blind on the lek in 10A on a number of occasions.

Ring-necked Pheasant, *Phasianus colchicus* Linnaeus

The pheasant is a common permanent resident. In winter, flocks frequent cultivated areas in the floodplain of lower Kings Creek; on 27 December 1983 as many as 40 birds were seen feeding in a stubble field. During the breeding season, birds move into uplands. Elmer Finck found a nest with 12 eggs on 3 May 1985 that had been destroyed by a controlled burn the day before. Chicks accompanied by hens have been observed in mid-June (13 June 1983). On 24 March 1985, Elmer Finck found a male pheasant being eaten by a red-tailed hawk just north of the main trail between 2C and N4D.

Greater Prairie-Chicken, *Tympanuchus cupido* (Linnaeus)

The prairie grouse is a common permanent resident, although in winter the birds are less frequently observed in upland prairie. There are nine perennially active leks on Konza Prairie, with an average of from 9 to 26 males per booming ground (Table 13 and

102

Fig. 21). As is typical for the species in the Flint Hills, birds' display areas are on ridge tops where grass is shorter as a result both of the activity of grazers and of the shallowness of the claypan soils. The maximum number of males recorded on a single lek was 35. All nests have been located in unburned prairie, and dates for nests with eggs range from late April (30 April) to mid-June (16 June). Fledged young accompanied by an adult have been seen as early as 27 May. Observed depredations of prairie-chickens on leks have involved Cooper's hawk, prairie falcon, peregrine falcon, and bobcat (*Lynx rufus*).

Wild Turkey, *Meleagris gallopavo* Linnaeus

Turkeys have become increasingly abundant in the Kansas River valley over the last five years. The first record for Konza Prairie was two females and four yearlings seen by Tim Seastedt and Cathy Tate in the wheat field along the entrance road on 28 March 1985. Subsequent records have been sporadic. Males were heard gobbling in the lower Kings Creek gallery forest during March and April of 1987, but no evidence was found of broods accompanied by females. There were no subsequent records from 4 May 1988 until the spring of 1992, when many observations were recorded. Of note is a record of one tom and 13 hens seen by Chris Smith behind the Hokansen house on 6 April. Dale Kennedy saw a hen and one chick in the Lower Shane Creek Valley on 11 June, and Deb Beutler found a nest with 10 eggs in prairie near the very top of the Shane Creek drainage on 18 June. There are two upland records from White Pasture: a bird seen by David Hartnett on 16 April 1987 and another along the north boundary on 3 April 1992.

Northern Bobwhite, *Colinus virginianus* (Linnaeus)

Numbers of this common permanent resident vary considerably from year to year. For example, in the fall of 1982 coveys were especially large, 25 to 30 birds being a minimum size. But late winter and early spring of 1983 were climatically severe (heavy

103

snows and cold temperatures), and birds became quite scarce, with no records at all for the month of March. And although birds were again recorded in mid-April, numbers remained low throughout the year. Yet in spite of these vagaries of winter conditions from year to year and their impacts on the population, June estimates of the population are relatively stable, with C.V.'s ranging between 11.5 and 50.9, except in the attenuated forest, where C.V. = 89.5. There are few nest records. A nest with eight eggs was discovered by Martha Hall on 18 July 1981, and Dean Stramel found a nest with just two eggs on 16 June 1987. Observations of recently fledged young are more numerous and span the period 23 June to 30 September.

Virginia Rail, *Rallus limicola* Vieillot

This rail is an occasional spring transient, discovered either by being flushed or being heard calling in response to taped calls from cattail swales in Pressee Branch or the middle fork of Swede Creek. Dates of record are from 8 April to 5 May. Birds are not present during periods of drought—for example, the spring of 1989.

Sora, *Porzana carolina* (Linnaeus)

The sora is also an occasional transient, primarily in spring from 7 April to 16 May, but it has occurred in fall (26 September 1985). Like the Virginia rail, the sora is found in marshy stretches of prairie streams, but it also has occurred at the upper end of Southgate Pond.

American Coot, *Fulica americana* Gmelin

The only records for this occasional transient are during April, when it has been observed on lower Kings Creek and Southgate Pond. The most surprising record is a bird flushed by Don Kaufman on 15 April 1984 along a mammal trap line in upland grass-land habitat.

Lesser Golden-Plover, *Pluvialis dominica* (Muller)

This transequatorial traveler is an uncommon spring transient from 23 April to 3 May. The lesser golden-plover is quite restricted in its habitat choice, selecting recently burned upland watersheds, where it often occurs in flocks of up to 50 individuals.

Killdeer, *Charadrius vociferus* Linnaeus

This plover is an uncommon summer resident and occasional winter visitor. It arrives in early March (3 March) and remains until late October (25 October), then becomes occasional from November through February. Killdeers are seldom seen in upland prairie, although they do forage in the spring on mowed areas such as fireguards, on the prairie-chicken lek open to the public in 10A, and on heavily grazed patches—for example, near the entrance gate to White Pasture. Similarly, Skinner et al. (1984) found this species to be most abundant on heavily grazed pastures; thus it is most regular in cultivated and disturbed areas along lower Kings Creek. The killdeer nests during April; the earliest breeding record is a nest with three eggs found by Elmer Finck on 4 April 1985. Fledged young have been seen as early as late April (30 April 1986) but are more commonly observed during May. During late summer they frequently visit margins of stock ponds.

Greater Yellowlegs, *Tringa melanoleuca* (Gmelin)

There is a single record on 18 April 1991 of a bird at a rain-filled depression in a recently burned watershed.

Lesser Yellowlegs, *Tringa flavipes* (Gmelin)

This sandpiper is an occasional spring transient from early April (6 April) to early May (10 May), usually seen flying in flocks low across the prairie or feeding at ponds (Southgate and N20A).

Solitary Sandpiper, *Tringa solitaria* Wilson

This species is an occasional visitor during migration at ponds (Westend, Texas Hog) during May (6–14 May) and late summer (31 July to 15 August). Latest date of record is 23 September 1991.

Willet, *Catoptrophorus semipalmatus* (Gmelin)

A single record was obtained for Southgate Pond on 25 April 1977.

Spotted Sandpiper, *Actitis macularia* (Linnaeus)

Spotties are occasional visitors during spring migration (30 April–8 May) and in late summer (26 July 1983) around ponds. There is one record of a bird flushed by Elmer Finck from the edge of the stream in 1A.

Upland Sandpiper, *Bartramia longicauda* (Bechstein)

Summer residents arrive in the second week of April (earliest date 5 April) and remain common until late July, when they begin to depart from the prairie. They are largely gone by the end of August. Migrants continue to pass over the prairie from farther north during September, with some site records during September and October. Latest date is 13 October. There are 31 nest records, all except one in watersheds that had not been burned that spring. The single nest in a burned watershed was started in mid-June (four eggs on 20 June 1979), well after the peak of nesting during the last two weeks of May. The earliest date is a nest that received its fourth egg on 6 May (1979) and fledged on 4 June, and the latest nest with eggs was found on 26 June (1978). Fledged young become frequent along trails and fireguards during the second week of June.

Marbled Godwit, *Limosa fedoa* (Linnaeus)

I have only a single record of this rare transient—a bird that set-
106 tled for a few moments by the rain-filled bison wallow in the

middle of the prairie-chicken lek in 10A on the morning of 12 April 1984. Although common in the prairie-pothole regions farther north, most individuals probably overfly the Flint Hills.

Long-billed Dowitcher, *Limnodromus scolopaceus* (Say)

This species is a rare transient, with only a single fall record on 8 October 1986.

Common Snipe, *Gallinago gallinago* (Linnaeus)

The snipe is an uncommon spring transient from 24 March until 19 May but is most frequently seen in April. It is found in the marshy swales in the Swede Creek drainage as well as in the east fork of Thowe Branch in N4C. There are two June records (25 June 1979 and 15 June 1983) and two fall records (2 October 1986 and 1 October 1991).

American Woodcock, *Scolopax minor* Gmelin

During the wet years from 1981 through 1987 this species became increasingly more regular during the breeding season in eastern and central Kansas. The first record on Konza Prairie was a displaying bird on 24 February 1984 heard by Elmer Finck, and the first summer record was a group of three birds that were seen flying on 19 June 1984 from the north fork of Kings Creek at dusk. During 1986 the species became uncommon, with many records from 27 March through 3 September. Latest fall record is 5 November. The first nest, containing two eggs, was discovered by Joe Gelroth near the Hokansen house on 28 April 1986. Displaying males could regularly be seen along the main trail in the brome field north of N20A and in the disturbed area around the old corral at the north end of N4D. In 1988 there was only a single record (8 April); as the drought intensified, there were no records for 1989, 1990, or 1991. During this dry period, earthworms were deep within the soil profile and unaccessible to woodcock (Sam James, personal communication).

107

Franklin's Gull, *Larus pipixcan* Wagler

This bird is a common migrant in spring from early April (9 April) to early May (4 May), with the latest date on 1 June. In fall the Franklin's gull occurs from 14 September to 29 October. It is most frequently seen flying low across the prairie feeding on aerial insects, but it is also attracted to recently burned watersheds. For example, on 22 April 1983 there were 64 individuals on 1B in upper Pressee Branch.

Ring-billed Gull, *Larus delawarensis* Ord

Like the Franklin's gull, this species is attracted to recently burned watersheds in spring. However, the ring-billed gull is much less frequently seen, being only occasional in spring (13 March to 23 April). There is a single fall record (31 October 1984).

Rock Dove, *Columba livia* Gmelin

Although recorded every week of the year, this uncommon permanent resident is restricted to the headquarters area and Hokansen house site, where it nests in man-made structures.

Mourning Dove, *Zenaida macoura* (Linnaeus)

The dove is an abundant summer resident from early March through the middle of September and remains common until early December. It is occasional from mid-December through February, since most of the population migrates farther south. The mourning dove nests on the ground in grassland habitats and in trees in the attenuated gallery forest and gallery forest edge. There are a total of 208 nest records, with the earliest nest with eggs on 8 April and the latest found by David Gibson on 9 September 1986. All early nests in April are on the ground. Although ground nests occur throughout the breeding season, the doves increasingly use trees beginning the last week of April. Nest placement ranges in height above the ground from 0.6 m to 2.5 m.

Black-billed Cuckoo, *Coccyzus erythropthalmus* (Wilson)

This species is an uncommon but regular summer resident in the rock outcrop community within grassland watersheds, a habitat quite different from the "heavy riparian shrubbery and second growth" reported by Johnston (1964) or the "denser, better-developed woodland" that Thompson and Ely (1989) identified as the preferred cover. Dates of occurrence range from 13 May to 14 October. I found a nest containing three eggs, 1.5 m up in a dogwood thicket on 31 May 1983. Greg Farley discovered a similarly placed nest with three eggs on 13 June 1986.

Yellow-billed Cuckoo, *Coccyzus americanus* (Linnaeus)

Noticeably more common than the previous species, the yellow-billed is present as a summer resident in riparian habitats from the main stems of Kings Creek and Shane Creek up to the ends of the attenuated gallery forest. Birds arrive in early May (4 May) and remain until early October (1 October). Elmer Finck found a nest with three eggs in an elm on 19 June 1984 and another with three eggs on 24 July 1985. A third, rather late nest, which subsequently failed, was discovered with two eggs in a hackberry on 28 August.

Barn Owl, *Tyto alba* (Scopoli)

Although there is only one record—a bird flushed from the upper watershed in 20B on 25 March 1981—this seldom-observed species is probably best described as an occasional visitor throughout the year.

Eastern Screech-Owl, *Otus asio* (Linnaeus)

This species is probably an occasional permanent resident, although there are only records for March, May, June, and November from lower Shane Creek, the main stem and the north fork of Kings Creek, and the forested valley in White Pasture.

109

CHAPTER SIX

Great Horned Owl, *Bubo virginianus* (Gmelin)

A hunter characteristic of more open habitat, this owl is an un-common permanent resident with records in almost every week of the year. There are three nest records. One nest, in the crown of a bur oak in the gallery forest along the main stem of Kings Creek, contained one young in natal down and a second young bird molting into juvenile plumage on 21 April 1982. On 9 May 1985, Dick Marzolf reported two young in a nest in a bur oak in the Kings Creek gallery forest that had been used in previous years by red-tailed hawks. The third nest, also in an old red-tailed hawk nest, was in a sycamore in the attenuated gallery forest in N2B. Recorded sightings include not only forested habi-tats but open grasslands. After the erection in the late 1980s of the native grazer fencing, horned owls have frequently perched on the sturdy posts along the periphery.

Burrowing Owl, *Speotyto cunicularia* (Molina)

On 27 April 1985 Bryan and Brenda Clark observed a burrowing owl in a grassland tract along the north fork of the Pressee Branch watershed that had been burned two weeks earlier. This is the only record of this rare migrant.

Barred Owl, *Strix varia* Barton

The typical owl of the eastern forest, this species is an uncom-mon permanent resident and is restricted to the gallery forests along the main stems of Kings and Shane creeks, probably with only a single pair in each valley. There are no nest records, but juvenile birds have been seen.

Long-eared Owl, *Asio otus* (Linnaeus)

The only record of this rare winter visitor is a bird seen by Craig Frank and Ron Klataske on 20 December 1986 along the main stem of Shane Creek.

110

Short-eared Owl, *Asio flammeus* (Pontoppidan)

This owl is an occasional migrant during late September (22 September) through mid-October (19 October) and in spring from early March through mid-April. It also occurs as a winter visitor in January and February. The short-eared owl is most regularly found in grassland watersheds that are burned on a 4- or 20-year cycle.

Common Nighthawk, *Chordeiles minor* (Forster)

The nighthawk is a common summer resident that usually arrives in early May. Most birds depart in August. Extreme dates are 30 April and 20 September. There are 32 nesting records, with egg dates ranging from 21 May to 19 July and young in nests from 29 June to 2 August. Nighthawks may be double brooded in annually burned plots, but only single brooded in grassland watersheds not burned in April of a given year. This behavior is probably a reflection of the removal of litter by spring burning, which makes this habitat more preferred because it provides the open nest sites required by this species. During fall migration roosting flocks of several dozen birds can be discovered along the edges of the gallery forest and upstream in attenuated gallery forest.

Common Poorwill, *Phalaenoptilus nuttallii* (Audubon)

The Flint Hills mark the eastern edge of this species' range in North America. This common summer resident arrives in mid-April and departs in September. Inclusive dates of record are from 8 April to 27 September. A nest with two young ready to fledge was found as early as 25 May, and a nest with eggs was discovered as late as 26 July. Deb Beutler discovered a nest with two young on 27 May 1992 from which the young departed on 11 June, moving 10 m away. All nests have been found along rocky outcrops in sparse vegetation, but common poorwills are most easily seen in summer at night along the main trail. On the 111 night of 17 August 1985, Elmer Finck counted 25 birds on 3 km of the main trail along the south fork of Kings Creek.

Chuck-will's-widow, *Caprimulgus carolinensis* Gmelin

This species is an uncommon summer resident in the forests along Kings and Shane creeks, arriving as early as 29 April. There is a single nest record in attenuated gallery forest associated with the north fork of Kings Creek. The nest contained two young on 2 July 1992. Fall departure is unknown for Konza Prairie (the latest date of record is 7 July) and for Kansas (Thompson and Ely 1989).

Whip-poor-will, *Caprimulgus vociferus* Wilson

This occasional transient in the gallery forest occurs from 30 April to 10 May, with a single fall record on 1 October 1986.

Chimney Swift, *Chaetura pelagica* (Linnaeus)

The chimney swift is a common summer resident that is restricted to the headquarters area, where it has been recorded nesting in the chimney of the Stonehouse in the headquarters area (a nestling fell into the basement fireplace on 20 August 1985). Inclusive dates are 18 April to 10 October.

Ruby-throated Hummingbird, *Archilochus colubris* (Linnaeus)

The species has been recorded as an occasional summer visitor but could be resident as a nesting species. Most records are probably transients during the period 15–22 May and again in the early fall, 15 August–2 September. There is one summer record: Don Kaufman observed a bird feeding on the trumpet vine flowers on the barn in the headquarters area on 17 July 1984.

Belted Kingfisher, *Ceryle alcyon* (Linnaeus)

The kingfisher has been observed every week of the year. It is an uncommon summer resident in lower Kings Creek as well as along the more perennial sections of streams throughout Konza

Prairie. The kingfisher is an occasional winter resident but restricted to open water along the main stem of Kings Creek. The only evidence of breeding has been the carrying of food by adults into assumed nest holes in clay banks of streams in early June.

Red-headed Woodpecker, *Melanerpes erythrocephalus* (Linnaeus)

This woodpecker is an abundant summer resident in the gallery forest, with a mean June population of 7.72 ± 0.93 birds/km. The species is significantly less common in the attenuated gallery forest (Student's t = 5.98, df = 18, P < 0.01), where June populations average 0.77 ± 0.30 birds/km. There is no relationship between summer populations in these two habitats; that is, when June gallery forest populations are high, they are not necessarily high in the attenuated gallery forest. Individuals can also be seen in isolated trees in upland prairie, but all nest records are from the two forest habitats. Copulations between birds have been noted in mid-May and fledged young observed in mid-July.

Winter populations are greater than summer populations in both habitats (11.24 ± 2.97 birds/km in the gallery forest and 1.69 ± 0.83 birds/km in the attenuated gallery forest), and the difference in relative abundances between the two habitats is maintained (Student's t = 3.10, df = 18, P < 0.01). Unlike June, however, in winter there is a significant correlation between populations in the two habitats (Pearson r = 0.72, N = 10, P < 0.01). This relationship is dependent on the importance of bur oak acorns as winter food, which would vary in abundance in both habitats. In summer, however, the availability of nest sites in the two habitats is probably the critical factor and should not be expected to vary in concert in both habitats.

There is considerable variation in the wintering population from year to year, ranging from 22.8 birds/km in the gallery forest in good acorn years to zero in years of mast crop failure when birds migrate to more suitable locations (Kendeigh 1982; Briggs et al. 1989). The coefficient of annual variation in the wintering   113 populations of the gallery forest (C.V. = 86.1) is over two times as great as in the more stable June populations (C.V. = 37.9). Again, this reflects the variation in the bur oak crop upon which the red-headed woodpecker is critically dependent in winter. Although the winter population is clearly a function of the abundance of bur oak mast (Smith 1986a), there is a significant positive correlation between the winter population in the gallery forest and the previous June population (Pearson $r = 0.60$, $N = 10$, $P < 0.05$), which suggests that when breeding populations are high, more birds remain over winter. But there is no correlation between the January population and the subsequent June population; that is, a good winter acorn crop does not result in a greater breeding population the next summer or a larger population the next winter (Smith 1986b). Obviously, many of these wintering birds go elsewhere to breed and may not return in the subsequent winter.

Red-bellied Woodpecker, *Melanerpes carolinus* (Linnaeus)

This species is a common permanent resident in the gallery forest. In summer its relative abundance in the gallery forest averages 1.48 ± 0.40 birds/km, a value significantly less than that of the red-headed woodpecker (Student's $t = 6.17$, $df = 18$, $P < 0.01$). Winter populations in the gallery forest average 1.85 ± 0.50 birds/km, an abundance that is also significantly different from that of the red-headed woodpecker (Student's $t = 3.12$, $df = 18$, $P < 0.01$). Abundances in the attenuated gallery forest of 0.92 ± 0.22 birds/km in summer and 1.00 ± 0.28 birds/km in winter are similar and no different from those of the red-headed woodpecker. Furthermore, there are no differences in red-bellied woodpecker densities between forest habitats or between seasons. The lack of seasonal difference was also the case for this species in more easterly prairie woodlots (Kendeigh 1982).

The red-bellied woodpecker is considerably more stable than the red-headed woodpecker (average C.V. for red-heads across all seasons and in all habitats equals 100.5 compared to 84.6 for the red-bellied); this stability reflects a broader, more reliable food resource base as well as the more generalist habitat requirements of the species (Kahl et al. 1985). But a competitive interaction between these two species during winter is suggested by Finck (1986), who demonstrated a negative correlation between their populations in the gallery forest.

Nesting begins in late May and early June, but the few nest records make defining the nesting season on Konza Prairie uncertain.

Yellow-bellied Sapsucker, *Sphyrapicus varius* (Linnaeus)

As an uncommon transient in the gallery forest and lower portions of the attenuated forest, the yellow-bellied sapsucker is more frequently seen in fall (24 October to 5 November) than in spring. There is only a single spring record (7 April 1987).

Downy Woodpecker, *Picoides pubescens* (Linnaeus)

This common permanent resident occurs in both the gallery forest and attenuated forest, but abundance in the gallery forest in January (2.10 ± 0.39 birds/km) is greater than it is in June (0.80 ± 0.36 birds/km) (Student's $t = 2.44$, df = 18, $P < 0.05$) as well as being greater than in the attenuated forest in January (0.92 ± 0.19 birds/km) (Student's $t = 2.70$, df = 18, $P < 0.01$). Abundances in the two forest communities during June show no differences. Birds are also present at low densities in shrubby vegetation on grassland sites during winter but not in summer. In the gallery forest, populations of downies are about twice as great as those of the larger hairy woodpecker. Courting birds are frequently seen, but there are no definite nest records.

Hairy Woodpecker, *Picoides villosus* (Linnaeus)

Much less obvious in its behavior than the downy, this species is frequent enough to be recorded every week of the year as an uncommon permanent resident in the gallery forest. In the attenu- 115 ated gallery forest it is present only during summer. Even though it most certainly breeds on Konza Prairie, there are no nest records.

Northern Flicker, *Colaptes auratus* (Linnaeus)

The yellow-shafted flicker (*C. a. auratus*) is a common permanent resident in both forested and grassland habitats, although birds seen in upland prairie during June are at densities less than a quarter of those in gallery forest. There is a significant difference between June populations in the gallery forest (2.28 ± 0.46 birds/km) and the attenuated forest (1.00 ± 0.20 birds/km) as well (Student's t = 2.55, df = 18, P < 0.05). There is no significant difference, however, in densities of populations in gallery and attenuated forest in January. In early spring (mid-March) birds are frequently flushed as they feed on the ground along the Jeep trails and mowed fireguards that form the boundaries between grassland burning treatments. In fall and winter flocks of from 10 to 15 individuals feeding on poison ivy are regular along lower Kings Creek. Nesting activity begins in mid-May, and fledged young being attended by adults have been observed by the last week in June.

From fall through spring, red-shafted flickers (*C. a. cafer*) are also present in low numbers on Konza Prairie. Inclusive dates are from 17 September to 15 April, but most records are during November.

Olive-sided Flycatcher, *Contopus borealis* (Swainson)

This flycatcher is conspicuous by its selection of snags above the forest canopy from which to make its feeding sallies. It is an uncommon transient along the edge of the gallery forest during a brief period in the last half of May (16–26 May), although there is one record as early as 4 May. Olive-sided flycatchers are more frequently seen from the middle of August to mid-September (earliest fall date is 31 July).

Eastern Wood-Pewee, *Contopus virens* (Linnaeus)

This common summer resident of the gallery forest and the contiguous attenuated forest does not occur in tree islands separated by intervening grassland. It is present from early May to September; inclusive dates are 5 May to 30 September. There are only two nest records, both from lower Kings Creek. One was placed 15 m up in a hackberry and fledged young on 27 July. The other was under construction 15 m up in a hackberry on 4 June.

Willow Flycatcher, *Empidonax trailii* (Audubon)

This species is a rare spring transient, passing through late in the period, although it probably migrates unnoticed in fall. There are just two dates for this period, 30 May 1985 and 6 June 1983, and both are from fields in early stages of forest succession, characterized by scattered small honey locust and elms. On 19 June 1992 a willow flycatcher was discovered singing in a cottonwood-willow-cattail slough in Pressee Branch, a situation suggestive of summer residency.

Least Flycatcher, *Empidonax minimus* (Baird and Baird)

From 4 May to 29 May and again from 2 September to 17 October, this bird is a common transient along the edge of the gallery forest and within the attenuated gallery forest. It is more frequently noted in spring because of its singing.

Eastern Phoebe, *Sayornis phoebe* (Latham)

An uncommon but regular nesting species, this summer resident arrives in mid-March and departs by mid-October; inclusive dates are 14 March to 14 October. Of the 17 nesting records, all but one are from sites in man-made structures (e.g., culverts, bridges, and barns). The one natural site was selected along lower Kings Creek just under the overhang of the stream bank, about 2 m above the water level. This nest was under construction on 12 April but subsequently abandoned before eggs were   117 laid. All nest records are from April and May, but the species is probably double brooded (Johnston 1964).

Great Crested Flycatcher, *Myiarchus crinitus* (Linnaeus)

This species is an abundant migrant and the most common resident flycatcher in forested habitats during summer. The inclusive dates of occurrence are from 24 April to 23 September. The mean relative abundance on June transects in the gallery forest is 8.09 ± 1.29 birds/km; abundance in the attenuated forest is 4.85 ± 0.71 birds/km. The difference between these means is significant (Student's $t = 2.20$, $df = 18$, $P < 0.05$). Nest-building activity is observed in late May, with birds using natural cavities as well as old woodpecker holes. One nest found by Steve Fretwell on 12 June 1981 was 5 m above the ground in the broken end of a dead snag and contained four young.

Western Kingbird, *Tyrannus verticalis* Say

The tallgrass prairie is not the habitat of primary choice for this species. It is only an occasional summer visitor, with individuals being found on sporadic dates at widely scattered sites. The few nesting records occurred in the disturbed habitat of the headquarters area. The first nest was discovered by Jenny Brazzle around 13 June 1990, 4.5 m above the ground in a hackberry. The adults were feeding young at this time. On 13 July Dave Sampson observed a second nest, being incubated by what was probably the same female, 15 m above the ground in an elm on the northwest side of the ranch house. A pair nested again in this elm during June 1991.

Eastern Kingbird, *Tyrannus tyrannus* (Linnaeus)

This kingbird is an abundant migrant, with first birds being recorded in spring during the last week in April (23 April) and last autumnal birds during September (22 September). During fall passage, which begins in mid-August, large, loose flocks of approximately 50 to 70 birds regularly stop over to feed primarily on dogwood berries and also on aerial insects. From May through July the eastern kingbird is a common breeding species. Of the 28 nests observed, most were placed from 2 to 9 m high in elms and honey locusts along the upper reaches of watercourses upstream from the terminus of the attenuated gallery forest. Occasionally a nest is placed in an isolated tree in upland prairie. Because of the choice of trees whose bark resists the quick passage of fires in annually burned prairie and whose branches are beyond the reach of the flames, the eastern kingbird and northern oriole are the only woody-dependent grassland species not significantly reduced in abundance by fire.

Scissor-tailed Flycatcher, *Tyrannus forficatus* (Gmelin)

Scissor-tails are occasional transients and summer visitors to Konza Prairie from late April (22 April) to mid-October (15 October). Like the western kingbird, scissor-tailed flycatchers have been found nesting only in atypical habitat. During 1987 a pair fledged three young from a nest 10 m above the ground in a hackberry next to the main weather station, and a pair nested in this same tree in 1988. Birds were feeding young on 5 July, but the eventual success of this nest was not determined. A third nest discovered in 1992 was placed 10 m high in an isolated hackberry in a field adjacent to the south fork of Kings Creek.

Horned Lark, *Eremophila alpestris* (Linnaeus)

Although Cody (1968) considered the horned lark as a component species in Flint Hills prairie, his data were biased from his inclusion of habitat on uplands heavily used by cattle. Skinner et al. (1984:16) more characteristically found the horned lark common in Missouri prairie only on "very short grasslands." Horned larks are occasional visitors on Konza Prairie from late February (21 February) until the end of May; during this time they are observed on mowed fireguards, prairie-chicken leks, or other claypan uplands that are characteristically vegetated by blue and hairy grama grasses in addition to the taller grasses. By

119

June, grass on most sites has grown tall enough and dense enough to exclude larks; there are only three later dates (7 June 1972, 22 June 1984, and 10 July 1981). A few larks return in late October (26 October) and linger through winter in appropriate habitat. There is only one breeding record, a nest under construction on 8 April 1983 that fledged one young during the first week of May. This nest was located on a ridge in White Pasture, an area that had been historically overgrazed and thus had a sparse cover of shortgrasses. Since that time White Pasture has been more moderately grazed, and larks have not returned to nest, although birds are classified as occasional there in early winter.

Purple Martin, *Progne subis* (Linnaeus)

An occasional transient and summer visitor from early April (7 April) to late summer, this swallow is most common in the period of fall departure during the last two weeks of August.

Tree Swallow, *Tachycineta bicolor* (Vieillot)

Although this species is a localized breeding bird in eastern Kansas, the only record for Konza Prairie is of a single bird flying over the brome field that borders the north side of the lower Kings Creek gallery forest on 4 May 1984.

Northern Rough-winged Swallow, *Stelgidopteryx serripennis* (Audubon)

This species is the only swallow that selects naturally occurring nesting sites in the tallgrass prairie. It is an uncommon summer resident, arriving in late March (27 March) and remaining until mid-August (17 August). There are two later dates for transients, 14 September 1983 and 10 October 1990. All nest sites are in clay banks of active streams, either within the gallery forest or along upper reaches of watersheds in prairie habitat.

Cliff Swallow, *Hirundo pyrrhonota* Vieillot

This swallow is an occasional summer visitor; inclusive dates are from 9 May to 12 September.

Barn Swallow, *Hirundo rustica* Linnaeus

Although an abundant transient, especially during mass flights in September, this swallow is a common summer visitor but only a localized nesting species. Inclusive dates of occurrence are from 8 April to 17 October. Nesting begins in early May and continues into July. All nests are within man-made structures (barns and other buildings and also under the old bridge on the highway 13 right-of-way in 2D).

Blue Jay, *Cyanocitta cristata* (Linnaeus)

The jay is a common permanent resident, being recorded in every week of the year. It is also an abundant transient, especially during autumnal migration; loose flocks of 50 to 180 have been observed during late September and early October.

June populations in the gallery forest average 7.28 ± 0.78 birds/km, which is significantly different from the average of 3.23 ± 0.42 birds/km in the attenuated gallery forest (Student's $t = 4.56$, $df = 18$, $P < 0.01$). Nest building begins in mid-April, and fledged young are present by mid-June. The species is single brooded and becomes considerably less obvious from late June until the beginning of fall migration.

During winter, gallery forest populations average 3.83 ± 1.29 birds/km, but this mean is not significantly different from the January average of 1.92 ± 0.76 birds/km in the attenuated gallery forest. The difference in the means for winter and summer populations in the gallery forest is significantly different (Student's $t = 2.29$, $df = 18$, $P < 0.05$), but the difference in the seasonal means for the attenuated gallery forest is not significantly different. The coefficients of variation of the populations in both habitats, however, are three times greater in winter (C.V. in January = 106.3 and 125.6 for the gallery and attenuated forest

121

respectively) than in summer (C.V. in June = 33.9 and 41.6 respectively), probably reflecting the variability of the acorn crop.

American Crow, *Corvus brachyrhynchos* Brehm

Crows are uncommon permanent residents with records for every week of the year. The species becomes common, however, from late August to early December, when flocks that may number as many as several hundred birds descend upon grassland tracts to feed. Since birds are relatively secretive during the breeding season, there are only two nest records. One nest was found 12 m above the ground in a chinquapin oak on 3 May 1989 along the north fork of Kings Creek, but its stage in the nesting cycle is not known. The second nest was being constructed 18 m above the ground in a bur oak on 16 March 1990 along Kings Creek near the Hokansen house. Active defense of nest sites by pairs of crows in response to human intrusion is experienced by many researchers in the gallery forest during early summer, even though the location of the nest sites is unknown.

Black-capped Chickadee, *Parus atricapillus* Linnaeus

The chickadee is a common permanent resident in both the gallery forest and attenuated gallery forest and frequently forages in the rock outcrop community within grassland sites. In forested habitats chickadees form the core of mixed-species flocks that develop in fall. These flocks attract migrants like orange-crowned and yellow-rumped warblers but are characterized in the winter months by titmouses, white-breasted nuthatches, brown creepers, golden-crowned kinglets, and downy woodpeckers.

Mean relative abundances of black-capped chickadees on June transects are 7.16 ± 1.33 birds/km in gallery forest and 3.92 ± 0.98 birds/km in attenuated gallery forest. In the winter, these values are 6.11 ± 1.19 birds/km and 3.92 ± 1.44 birds/km, respectively. None of these means is significantly different between habitats or between seasons, the measured chickadee populations being similar, especially within habitats. The annual stability of these populations is greater in June (C.V. = 58.9 and 79.3 in gallery forest and attenuated forest, respectively) than in January (C.V. = 61.8 and 116.1, respectively).

There are no nest records prior to 1 April, and all sites have been old woodpecker holes in chinquapin oaks, 4 to 6 m above the ground. Adults feeding young are quite obvious throughout May, and Greg Farley observed an adult feeding fledglings as late as 13 June 1987 in the attenuated gallery forest along the Thowe Branch.

Tufted Titmouse, *Parus bicolor* Linnaeus

Having been recorded during every week of the year, the titmouse is a common permanent resident. In contrast to chickadees, however, the tufted titmouse is restricted to forest sites. Its population is significantly higher in the gallery forest than in the attenuated gallery forest (Student's $t = 5.21$, $df = 18$, $P < 0.01$ in June; Student's $t = 3.13$, $df = 18$, $P < 0.01$ in January) and significantly higher in summer than in winter in the gallery forest (Student's $t = 3.06$, $df = 18$, $P < 0.01$) but not in the attenuated forest. Relative abundances in the gallery forest are 4.07 ± 0.59 birds/km on June transects and 1.79 ± 0.46 birds/km in January. In the attenuated gallery forest, there are 0.69 ± 0.27 birds/km on June transects and 0.31 ± 0.13 birds/km in January. This preference for forests is reflected in the analysis by Kahl et al. (1985) that demonstrated habitat correlations in forests with a canopy height of 12 to 24 m and canopies that are at least 75 percent closed. Nest building has been observed as early as 27 March, and adults have been seen feeding fledged young during the first two weeks of June. The only nest site discovered was a late nest (28 June 1989) located in the broken stub of a bur oak along the north fork of Kings Creek, 12 m above the ground.

Red-breasted Nuthatch, *Sitta canadensis* Linnaeus

The scarcity of conifers provides inappropriate habitat for the red-breasted nuthatch. This species is therefore a rare transient, with only a single date of presence on 13 October 1989.

123

White-breasted Nuthatch, *Sitta carolinensis* Latham

The white-breasted nuthatch is a common permanent resident, being present every week of the year. The habitat distribution of this nuthatch is similar to that of the titmouse in that populations are higher in the gallery forest than in the attenuated gallery forest in both summer (4.51 ± 0.84 birds/km versus 2.07 ± 0.98 birds/km) and winter (2.90 ± 0.56 birds/km versus 1.23 ± 0.43 birds/km) but only significantly different in January (Student's $t = 2.36$, df = 18, $P < 0.05$). There is no difference between winter and summer populations in either habitat. Only one nest record has been obtained. This involved a female bringing nest material to a hole that was 6 m above the ground in a bur oak along Shane Creek on 1 April 1981.

Brown Creeper, *Certhia americana* Bonaparte

The creeper is an uncommon transient and winter resident in the gallery forest from the second week in October to the last week in April; inclusive dates are 1 October to 29 April. The species has been recorded only once on January transects in the attenuated gallery forest. In some winters it is abundant in the gallery forest (7.41 birds/km in 1990), but it is completely absent in other winters. Furthermore, its numbers vary abruptly during winter. In the winter of 1981–1982 brown creepers were present in November and December but then gone in January. But in 1982–1983, the species did not arrive as a winter resident until January and even then densities were low (1.23 birds/km). In the winter of 1989–1990, on the other hand, birds were abundant up until the first week of January and then absent until the last week in March, when a noticeable influx of migrants appeared on 30 March 1990.

Rock Wren, *Salpinctes obsoletus* (Say)

There is only one record for this species, which breeds in Kansas from the Smoky Hills westward. A single bird was seen on 12

October 1982, appropriately in a rocky cut along the old highway 13 right-of-way in Texas Hog pasture.

Carolina Wren, *Thryothorus ludovicianus* (Latham)

Populations of the Carolina wren are depressed by winters of low temperature and heavy snow cover (Kendeigh 1982), and Kansas populations of this permanent resident were substantially reduced by a succession of adverse winters during the mid-1970s. Thus the species was largely extirpated in the Flint Hills before the acquisition of the forest habitats of Konza Prairie in 1977. The first record for Konza Prairie was a bird seen by Judy Bogusch along Shane Creek on 18 December 1982. The species reappeared in the late summer of 1983 (17 August) and was present until late October. But the winter of 1983–1984 was also harsh, and the species was again eliminated from the site. The next record was a 7 April 1987 sighting by Elmer Finck, but there appeared to be no established population that summer. There was another late summer record on 27 August 1987, and then by the summer of 1988 the species had become reestablished, increasing in numbers through 1990. In the last week of October 1990 there were four singing males along just 200 m of the bird transect in lower Kings Creek. Carolina wrens were not recorded on June transects in gallery forest until 1992.

Although no nests have been found, mated territorial birds have been seen during the breeding season along lower Kings Creek, the north fork of Kings Creek, and Shane Creek. On 26 April 1989, I observed a female with an obvious brood patch preening along Kings Creek just downstream from the nature trail crossing. At the present time, I consider the Carolina wren to be an uncommon permanent resident in the gallery forest.

Bewick's Wren, *Thryomanes bewickii* (Audubon)

From the first week in March until the last week in August, the Bewick's wren is a common summer resident in the attenuated gallery forest. There it establishes territories in patches charac-   125 terized by low numbers of trunks, high canopy levels, greater canopy cover, and a large percentage of standing dead snags (Farley 1987). It forages, but does not nest, in the rock outcrop community. Numbers progressively decrease through September and October, but a few birds remain during most years, so that the species is an occasional winter resident until numbers again increase during migration in March.

Greg Farley (1987) reported on the basis of seven nests that initial nesting begins in early April with fledging in mid-May. Three-quarters of the females begin second broods in late May that fledge in late June, although there is a nest-building date as late as 14 June 1987. All nests are located within cavities in dead snags. Dale Kennedy put out a series of nest boxes along the edge of the Shane Creek gallery forest in 1991 in hopes of attracting house wrens. No house wrens used the boxes, since it was a little late in the season. Instead she got five Bewick's wrens, since it was coincident with timing of the initiation of second broods. Of these five clutches, 80 percent were successful, producing 20 fledglings (67 percent of all eggs laid).

House Wren, *Troglodytes aedon* Vieillot

This species is an abundant summer resident. It arrives in April and remains abundant until the end of August; numbers then decline as birds depart until they are gone by the second week in October (inclusive dates are 5 April to 12 October). House wrens are present in both gallery forest and attenuated gallery forest, and there is no significant difference in relative abundance between habitats (3.58 ± 1.01 birds/km and 2.92 ± 0.69 birds/km, respectively). The species is also present in isolated woody patches within unburned grassland watersheds, resulting in a relative abundance (1.33 ± 0.29 birds/km) that is significantly different (Student's $t = 2.14$, df $= 18$, $P < 0.05$) from its abundance in both forest habitats. House wrens nest in dead trees, using both old woodpecker holes and natural cavities like the broken ends of limbs for nest sites. Nests are usually between 3 and

10 m above the ground. One nest, however, was discovered by Martha Hall on 10 July 1981 in a hole in a silver-painted metal corral post along the south fork of Kings Creek.

Winter Wren, *Troglodytes troglodytes* (Linnaeus)

The winter wren is an occasional transient and winter resident. It occurs most frequently within the gallery forest along the lower reaches of the creeks where stream cutting has produced exposed banks and floods have deposited piles of debris. Dates of occurrence span the period from 27 September to 13 April.

Sedge Wren, *Cistothorus platensis* (Latham)

This wren is an occasional spring transient during late April and early May (23 April to 15 May). It then returns in July (earliest date, 30 June) in years of adequate rainfall to nest in grassland burned that spring as well as in unburned prairie. This temporal pattern is also characteristic of the tallgrass prairies of western Missouri (Skinner et al. 1984). There is one record, 5 June 1986, during the intervening period. Autumnal departure is during September and October, with the last date of record on 24 October. In the drought years of 1988 and 1989, when primary productivity was depressed during the growing season, sedge wrens were not present in late summer. Males have been observed building nests, but the only evidence for breeding was an adult with food seen by Elmer Finck on 27 August 1985 to enter the vegetation. The bird gave vigorous distraction displays, but the nest or fledged young were never found.

Marsh Wren, *Cistothorus palustris* (Wilson)

This rare transient occurs in cattail swales in upland prairie, but it has only been seen in fall on two occasions: 14 September 1983 and 2 October 1984.

127

Golden-crowned Kinglet, *Regulus satrapa* Lichtenstein

During spring passage this species is occasional, being present from 16 March through 13 April. The golden-crowned kinglet is an uncommon winter resident in the gallery forest, joining chickadees as a member of mixed-species flocks. Mean relative abundance on January transects in the gallery forest is 2.22 ± 0.67 birds/km; this species has never been counted on the attenuated gallery forest transect. Birds regularly arrive in October (earliest date, 9 October) and typically remain through December, but in most years they depart in January. There are February dates only for 1982, 1983, 1988, and 1989. I suspect that the variability in their departure is related to availability of food, which requires that birds seek sustenance elsewhere before the onset of the vernal migration.

Ruby-crowned Kinglet, *Regulus calendula* (Linnaeus)

The surprisingly loud and complex song of this small, hyperactive bird announces its spring arrival. It is a common transient in spring from 21 March to 12 May and in fall from 9 September to 5 November. During mid-October ruby-crowned kinglets are often abundant along the forest edge in both gallery forest and attenuated gallery forest. Elmer Finck saw a late spring bird on 10 June 1982. There is a single winter record on 17 December 1987, when I saw a ruby-crown searching among the roots under the snow-free overhang of the bank along lower Kings Creek.

Blue-gray Gnatcatcher, *Polioptila caerulea* (Linnaeus)

This species is an uncommon but regular summer resident in the gallery forest along Kings and Shane creeks. Birds usually arrive in early April and remain until mid-September (inclusive dates are 31 March to 17 September), although they are inconspicuous after mid-July. Nest construction has been observed during the last week of April through the first week of May. Nests are most frequently placed in hackberry, but elm and walnut have also been used. Height of nest placement ranges from 11 to 15 m.

Fledged young have been observed in mid-June, but there is an observation of adults feeding fledglings as late as 9 August.

Eastern Bluebird, *Sialia sialis* (Linnaeus)

This bluebird is a common summer resident from early March on but then becomes an uncommon winter resident from December until the end of February. There is no direct evidence that any of the summer population remains in winter, but I suspect that most winter birds are local breeding birds. Yet during some winters—for example, 1982–1983—bluebirds are noticeably absent. In summer the eastern bluebird is restricted to forested habitats, but in fall flocks can be found above the attenuated gallery forest in the rock outcrop community.

Nest building has been first observed on 21 March, and fledged young being fed by adults have been seen as early as 10 June. Nest sites are both within the gallery forest interior and at the forest edge. Old woodpecker holes and natural cavities in dead tree boles or branches are used; nest heights range from 3 to 15 m above the ground. From 1986 through 1988 bluebirds regularly used an old woodpecker hole 1 m above the ground in a gate post adjacent to the weather station in the headquarters area, well away from forest patches. Johnston (1964) considered this species to be double brooded in Kansas; in some years there may be even more than two broods produced.

Mountain Bluebird, *Sialia currucoides* (Bechstein)

This visitor from the western mountains is a rare vagrant, although it is an uncommon but regular winter resident as far east as the Smoky Hills. There are two records: a single bird observed with a group of eastern bluebirds on 8 April 1986 by Chris Smith and a flock of six birds seen by Elmer Finck on 17 January 1989.

Veery, *Catharus fuscescens* (Stephens)

There is a single record on 18 May 1982 of a bird seen within the interior of the gallery forest along lower Kings Creek.

129

Gray-cheeked Thrush, *Catharus minimus* (Lafresnaye)

Although the gray-cheeked thrush is probably a more frequent transient than the veery, there are only two records for this rare migrant. The first was on 14 May 1981 within the gallery forest along the north fork of Kings Creek and the second on 11 May 1989 along lower Kings Creek.

Swainson's Thrush, *Catharus ustulatus* (Nuttall)

This thrush is an uncommon transient in forest and forest edge habitats during spring; dates of presence span the period 29 April to 1 June, but most records are during the first two weeks of May. In fall it is occasional, with only a single record on 17 September 1985.

Hermit Thrush, *Catharus guttatus* (Pallas)

There are no spring dates for this occasional transient and few dates during fall passage (6 October 1982, 26 October 1983, 13 October 1989).

Wood Thrush, *Hylocichla mustelina* (Gmelin)

The wood thrush is an occasional migrant, having been seen in May (4 May 1987) and October (17 October 1983).

American Robin, *Turdus migratorius* Linnaeus

Although winter and summer populations are certainly different birds, there are records for the robin in every week of the year. It is a common summer resident from March through August; numbers of birds seen during fall passage and winter, however, are directly related to availability of fruit. In fall of 1982, for example, the dogwood crop was excellent, and there were flocks of hundreds of robins in the attenuated gallery forest and rock outcrop communities in late October. Numbers reached the "thousands" in early November in the gallery forest of both the north and south forks of Kings Creek. Since dogwood is depleted during fall migration, being especially attractive to eastern kingbirds as well as to robins, availability of hackberry fruit is the primary determinant of robins' presence from late November through February. When the hackberry crop is sufficient, robins will be abundant in the gallery forest. During the spring of 1986, a caterpillar outbreak defoliated most hackberries; although they leafed out again, the fruit crop was sparse, and robins were gone from the gallery forest by the end of January. In years when hackberry flowers are frozen in spring and no fruit is produced, as in 1987, robins become infrequent in winter. Hackberry fruits were abundant in the winter of 1988–1989, and the January transect in the gallery forest tallied 22.2 birds/km! In 1989, not only was there a spring freeze that eliminated hackberry fruits but also the continuing drought affected production of dogwood fruit. Robins consequently were scarce after the end of September, although small flocks could be found in the gallery forest during fall migration feeding on poison ivy berries.

Nest building has been observed from early May to mid-June, and fledged young attended by an adult have been observed in June and July. Most nests have been discovered in gallery forest and attenuated gallery forest, but some robins use man-made structures in the headquarters area.

Gray Catbird, *Dumetella carolinensis* (Linnaeus)

The catbird is an uncommon summer resident from late April until the middle of October, occurring most frequently at the upper ends of the attenuated gallery forest and in denser rock outcrop communities. During some years (e.g., 1983), however, they are scarce. Extreme dates of record are 6 April to 17 October. There are only two nesting records: a nest with four young on 26 June 1982 and a nest with two eggs on 23 June 1982. Adults feeding fledged young have been observed during the first week in July.

Northern Mockingbird, *Mimus polyglottos* (Linnaeus)

The mockingbird is less common in the Flint Hills than in regions of Kansas to the east and to the west. On Konza Prairie this species is an uncommon spring and fall visitor, an occa-

131

sional summer visitor, and a rare winter visitor. It has most frequently been observed in the rock outcrop shrub community of
Texas Hog pasture.

Brown Thrasher, *Toxostoma rufum* (Linnaeus)

This abundant summer resident occurs in all habitats. It is significantly less common in the gallery forest (0.62 ± 0.20 birds/km)
than in the attenuated gallery forest (2.08 ± 0.43 birds/km; Student's t = 3.06, df = 18, P < 0.01). In grassland habitats that provide rock outcrop vegetation or where suitable nesting trees and
shrubs occur along the drainage channels, the brown thrasher's
abundance (2.79 ± 0.23 birds/km) equals that in the attenuated
forest. Thrashers are present from early April until mid-October;
inclusive dates are 31 March to 15 October. Most of the 53 nesting records are in small trees (elm, Osage orange, and red cedar)
or shrubs (dogwood, prickly ash, American plum), but one nest
with five eggs was on the ground. The thrasher is single
brooded, with most egg-laying occurring in mid-May (Johnston
1964), but birds have been observed in nest-building activities as
late as 30 June. Fledged young have been observed as early as 13
June.

American Pipit, *Anthus spinoletta* (Linnaeus)

This pipit is an occasional spring transient during a short period
from the last week in April through the first week in May, when
flocks can be found on recently burned upland prairie. Fall dates
range from 22 September to 17 October; during that time birds
frequent the margins of ponds or are flushed from along the
Jeep trails.

Sprague's Pipit, *Anthus spragueii* (Audubon)

There are only two records for this rare transient, both in the first
week of October. Steve Fretwell found one bird in 1978 in short-
132   grass adjacent to the old corral on the south fork of Kings Creek,

and Elmer Finck observed another single bird in 1985 along the main trail on the east side of 4D.

Cedar Waxwing, *Bomycilla cedrorum* Vieillot

Although this species nests occasionally in eastern Kansas (Johnston 1964), it only occurs on Konza Prairie as an uncommon spring transient and an occasional but highly erratic winter visitor in the gallery forest and the attenuated gallery forest. Spring dates range from 16 March until 17 May, and birds do not occur again until early November (2 November), although there is a record of a small flock along lower Kings Creek on 2 September 1991. Some winters the waxwings remain only until January; other years they linger until spring.

Loggerhead Shrike, *Lanius ludovicianus* Linnaeus

The shrike is an uncommon resident from March through late November, after which it becomes occasional December through February. It occurs in upland prairie where fence posts or isolated trees provide perches. Shrikes are also present in disturbed sites along the main trail on the north side of N20A, where Elmer Finck obtained the first breeding record, a nest placed 1.5 m above the ground in a honey locust. This nest contained six eggs on 10 May 1983 and fledged four young on 13 June. A second nest was discovered 3 m up in an elm on the first terrace of the watershed in N4D on 6 June 1991. This nest contained four eggs and eventually fledged at least one young. Fledged young accompanied by adults were also observed during the first week in June 1983 in the southwest corner of 20A and in 20B on 23 June 1990. The species probably nests every year in this area.

European Starling, *Sturnus vulgaris* Linnaeus

The starling is a common permanent resident with records for every week of the year. As a breeding species it not only nests in man-made structures in the headquarters area but uses old woodpecker holes and natural cavities in standing dead and live

133

trees throughout the gallery forest and attenuated gallery forest. Nest building begins in April, but data on nest histories are few. In fall and again in spring the starling occasionally gathers in flocks of over a hundred individuals to feed in upland prairie.

White-eyed Vireo, *Vireo griseus* (Boddaert)

This vireo is a rare spring transient (7 May 1989) and late summer visitor (16 July 1982, 27 July 1983) in dogwood thickets along rock outcrops.

Bell's Vireo, *Vireo bellii* Audubon

Johnston (1964) considered this species to be common in riparian thickets and second-growth scrub, but on Konza Prairie the Bell's vireo is the definitive species of the dogwood thickets associated with rock outcrops and seeps in prairie habitat. This general pattern of habitat selection also is typical for this species in Missouri (Kahl et al. 1985). Bell's vireos arrive in the first week of May and depart by early October (extreme dates 4 May to 24 October).

This common summer resident selects sites within the interior of dogwood clumps where stem density is great and the canopy is less than 6 m high. It builds its nest between two live stems about 1 m above the ground and below the canopy of leaves. Most nests are in dogwood, but others have been placed in honey locust and plum growing within the interior of dogwood thickets. The 40 nests of 17 pairs studied by Greg Farley (1987) ranged in date from 22 May (earliest egg date) to 15 August (latest fledging date). The species is single brooded and nests coincidentally with the peak in cowbird reproduction (Zimmerman 1983); abandonment in response to cowbird social parasitism is thus the major cause of nest failure (49 percent of nests lost, Farley 1987).

Solitary Vireo, *Vireo solitarius* (Wilson)

This transient is occasional during the first week in May and un-common during the period of fall passage, ranging from 16 September to 13 October. During that time it can be found along the edge of the gallery forest or within the attenuated gallery forest.

Warbling Vireo, *Vireo gilvus* (Vieillot)

There are few cottonwood stands on Konza Prairie; it is therefore not surprising that the warbling vireo is an uncommon summer resident. Birds arrive in mid-April and remain until late September (extreme dates 6 April to 1 October) and are most regularly found along the east fork of Swede Creek in 20C and the north edge of the gallery forest of lower Kings Creek. Although this species probably nests, there have been no breeding records.

Red-eyed Vireo, *Vireo olivaceus* (Linnaeus)

This vireo is an uncommon summer resident in the gallery forests along lower Kings Creek and Shane Creek, but there is no evidence for nesting. Birds arrive in early May and remain until early September, but they are difficult to locate after the end of July. Inclusive dates are 3 May to 8 September.

Tennessee Warbler, *Vermivora peregrina* (Wilson)

The Tennessee warbler is a common transient throughout May, although most dates are from the first two weeks of the month. There are no fall records, but I suspect it is overlooked rather than absent.

Orange-crowned Warbler, *Vermivora celata* (Say)

Orange-crowns are common transients during both spring (24 April to 15 May) and fall (16 September to 26 October). Although most frequently seen along the edge of the gallery forest and in the attenuated gallery forest, this species can be expected in prairie in the rock outcrop community and in isolated upland patches of dogwood, plum, and elm.

135

Nashville Warbler, *Vermivora ruficapilla* (Wilson)

The Nashville warbler is perhaps a little less abundant than the orange-crowned, but it is still a common transient in spring and fall in the same habitats as orange-crowns and yellow-rumps. Spring dates of occurrence range from 27 April to 15 May, and for fall the dates are from 27 August to 31 October.

Northern Parula, *Parula americana* (Linnaeus)

It is unclear whether this species actually nests in the gallery forest along lower Kings Creek or whether it is just an occasional summer visitor from farther downstream, where it is a summer resident along McDowell Creek. The earliest spring date is 25 April, and the latest fall date is 1 September. There are three recent summer dates: 28 June 1989, 11 July 1989, and 21 June 1990. Perhaps with the slow change in the gallery forest from domination by bur oak to a more mixed floodplain forest, parulas are beginning to invade this habitat. The analysis by Kahl et al. (1985) in Missouri suggested, however, that it might be less a function of forest species diversity than the increase in canopy height (not less than 20 m) and increased canopy coverage (at least 70 percent).

Yellow Warbler, *Dendroica petechia* (Linnaeus)

Although this species is a summer resident in the region, it is only an uncommon transient and occasional late summer visitor to Konza Prairie. Dates of vernal passage range from 4 May to 23 May, with two additional records in June (13 June 1985 and 5 June 1986). The species returns to Konza Prairie in August and is present until early September; inclusive dates are 17 August to 5 September.

Chestnut-sided Warbler, *Dendroica pensylvanica* (Linnaeus)

This warbler is a rare spring migrant with only two dates of record: 15 May 1978 and 15 May 1987.

Magnolia Warbler, *Dendroica magnolia* (Wilson)

This species is a rare transient during mid-May (9 May 1983, 19 May 1981) and in October (17 October 1983).

Yellow-rumped Warbler, *Dendroica coronata* (Linnaeus)

The most frequent dates of record for this common spring transient are throughout April until the first week in May, although it has been seen as early as 21 March and as late as 12 May. In fall the yellow-rumped warbler is sometimes abundant during the period of peak migration in October. Inclusive dates for fall passage are from 26 September to 11 November. The species is present across a broad range of woody habitats, from clumps of dogwood in upland prairie to within the interior of the gallery forest. It frequently associates in mixed-species flocks with chickadees, titmouses, kinglets, and orange-crowned warblers.

Black-throated Green Warbler, *Dendroica virens* (Gmelin)

This warbler is an occasional transient that is most frequently seen during October along the edge of the gallery forest.

Blackburnian Warbler, *Dendroica fusca* (Müller)

On 9 May 1983 there were many Blackburnian warblers in the gallery forest of lower Kings Creek, but it is usually only an occasional transient in May (latest date, 29 May) and early September.

Pine Warbler, *Dendroica pinus* (Wilson)

This is a rare spring transient, with the only records for Konza Prairie on 21 March and 10 April in 1986.

Palm Warbler, *Dendroica palmarum* (Gmelin)

There are only three fall records for this rare transient. Two were in 1981 (27 September and 4 October), when birds were seen along the edge of the attenuated gallery forest and in an isolated woody island, both in the drainage of the south fork of Kings

137

Creek. The third was on 1 October 1991 along the main stem of Kings Creek near the nature trail crossing.

Bay-breasted Warbler, *Dendroica castanea* (Wilson)

There is only one record for this rare transient, a bird seen along the edge of the gallery forest in lower Kings Creek on 2 September 1987.

Blackpoll Warbler, *Dendroica striata* (Forster)

This species is an occasional spring transient during the first two weeks of May, but there are no fall records.

Black-and-White Warbler, *Mniotilta varia* (Linnaeus)

The dates of spring passage for this uncommon transient span the period from 30 March to 19 May, but there are occasional summer records during late May and throughout June that suggest that this species may be a summer resident in the attenuated gallery forest in both the Kings Creek and Shane Creek watersheds. Kahl et al. (1985) have demonstrated that a dense shrub layer and a well-developed ground layer are correlated with this species' breeding presence, and the attenuated gallery forest comes close to matching this vegetative structure. Johnston (1964) listed breeding records for this species along the southern border of the state as far west as Sedgwick County. Fall movement begins in mid-August, and the species becomes an uncommon migrant from 31 August to 1 October.

American Redstart, *Setophaga ruticilla* (Linnaeus)

This species is an uncommon transient during the first two weeks of May (4–15 May) and from late August to early October (28 August–1 October).

Ovenbird, *Seiurus aurocapillus* (Linnaeus)

All spring dates for this uncommon transient are during the first three weeks of May (4–19 May), and there is only a single fall record (18 September 1984). The ovenbird is most frequently seen within the interior of the gallery forest along lower Kings Creek, but it has occurred in the dense dogwood stands adjacent to the cattail swale on upper Pressee Branch.

Louisiana Waterthrush, *Seiurus motacilla* (Vieillot)

The Louisiana waterthrush is an uncommon summer resident in the gallery forest along Shane Creek, lower Kings Creek, the north fork of Kings Creek upstream to the Jeep trail crossing between K20A and K4A, and the south fork of Kings Creek to just upstream of the Brunker homestead. Birds arrive during the first week of April and remain until the first week of September; inclusive dates are 2 April to 3 September.

There are two nest records. Steve Fretwell found a nest containing five waterthrush young, two cowbird nestlings, and two waterthrush eggs on 18 June 1978 along lower Kings Creek. The second nest was also along lower Kings Creek and was being built in a cavelike cavity in the clay bank on 21 and 26 April 1989. On 6 May the nest contained two waterthrush eggs and two cowbird eggs. Fledging occurred around 22 May, but the only evidence of success was an observation of an adult feeding an almost independent cowbird on 21 June, about 150 m downstream from the nest site.

Kentucky Warbler, *Oporornis formosus* (Wilson)

Although there are no breeding records for this species, it is probably an occasional summer resident in the gallery forest of lower Kings Creek and the north fork of Kings Creek. During 1982, 1983, and 1989, however, it was absent. Dates of record are from 14 May to 31 August.

Mourning Warbler, *Oporornis philadelphia* (Wilson)

There are only three records for this occasional transient: 1 June 1983, 11 September 1984, and 1 October 1986.

Common Yellowthroat, *Geothlypis trichas* (Linnaeus)

This common summer resident arrives during the middle of April and remains until the first week of October; extreme dates are 10 April to 14 October. Yellowthroats are restricted to grassland drainages, swales, and seeps at sites where the soil remains moist. Furthermore, they are most dense in unburned prairie, where they occur at an average relative abundance of 3.08 ± 0.39 birds/km on June transects. Although occasionally recorded on transects in annually burned watersheds, numbers average only 0.25 ± 0.17 birds/km. The only breeding record is the observation of both adults repeatedly carrying food to a spot in heavy buckbrush on 6 June 1983, but the nest or fledged young were never discovered.

Wilson's Warbler, *Wilsonia pusilla* (Wilson)

This species is an occasional spring transient during the first two weeks of May and an uncommon fall transient from late August (24 August) until late September (30 September).

Yellow-breasted Chat, *Icteria virens* (Linnaeus)

Although the chat breeds in localized areas throughout Kansas (Johnston 1964), it is a rare spring transient at Konza Prairie. There is only a single record of a singing bird in the oldfield east of Kings Creek along the northern boundary on 15 May 1978.

Summer Tanager, *Piranga rubra* (Linnaeus)

Although no evidence for nesting has been obtained, I have no doubts that this uncommon summer resident breeds in the gallery forest and attenuated gallery forest in both the Kings Creek and Shane Creek drainages. The species arrives in early May and departs in late September; extreme dates are 24 April and 4 October.

Scarlet Tanager, *Piranga olivacea* (Gmelin)

This tanager is an uncommon transient during May, is an occasional summer visitor in the gallery forest, and may even nest. The latest date is a male in molt observed on 11 August.

Northern Cardinal, *Cardinalis cardinalis* (Linnaeus)

The cardinal is a common permanent resident, recorded during every week of the year. In winter it is most frequent in oldfields associated with the forest edge of the gallery forest. In fall, especially in years of good dogwood production, it can be found in woody patches in upland prairie feeding on fruit. Nesting habitat extends from the gallery forest through the upper end of the attenuated gallery forest. Peak nesting activity occurs in spring, with nest building observed as early as the third week of April; as Johnston (1964) noted, nesting continues throughout summer. The latest date for nest building is 14 July at a site in the attenuated gallery forest on the main stem of Shane Creek.

Rose-breasted Grosbeak, *Pheucticus ludovicianus* (Linnaeus)

This species is a common transient during late April and early May but only occasional during fall passage (latest date, 14 October). Grosbeaks are uncommon summer residents in the gallery forest from May through August, but there are no nest records.

Blue Grosbeak, *Guiraca caerulea* (Linnaeus)

Largely restricted to the attenuated gallery forest and rock outcrop communities, this grosbeak is an uncommon summer resident. There is no evidence for breeding except for a copulating pair on 4 June 1991. Inclusive dates of occurrence are 4 May to 31 August.

Lazuli Bunting, *Passerina amoena* (Say)

This species is a rare transient observed only once, 15 May 1985, along the edge of the lower Kings Creek gallery forest near the Hokansen house.

141

Indigo Bunting, *Passerina cyanea* (Linnaeus)

The indigo bunting is a common transient in spring when it arrives in early May (earliest date, 4 May) and again in fall during September (latest date, 1 October). It is an uncommon summer resident in the gallery forest and the attenuated gallery forest. There is a single breeding record, a nest being built 0.6 m above the ground in a small hackberry in the understory of the Kings Creek gallery forest on 1 June 1983. On 13 June the nest contained three eggs, but it was depredated during the next week.

Dickcissel, *Spiza americana* (Gmelin)

Although the dickcissel prefers oldfield habitats rather than prairie (Zimmerman 1971), it is still the most common territorial species during summer in tallgrass prairie. Relative abundances are similar in unburned watersheds (13.94 ± 0.90 birds/km) and annually burned prairie (12.34 ± 1.86 birds/km). The species arrives in prairie habitat in early May (earliest date, 30 April) but does not become abundant until the end of May. There are 125 nesting records for Konza Prairie. Although nests have been started as early as the last week in May, the peak for nest starts is during the third week of June (Zimmerman 1984). The breeding population departs during late August and September, but a molting female was still present in upland prairie on 9 October. Transient flocks occur during late September and October in the taller grass along prairie drainages and in the rock outcrop community (latest date, 23 October).

Rufous-sided Towhee, *Pipilo erythrophthalmus* (Linnaeus)

This species occurs all year long on Konza Prairie, but breeding birds are *P. e. erythrophthalmus*, whereas wintering individuals are *P. e. maculatus*. The breeding population arrives in early April and departs in late September; extreme dates are 27 March and 19 October. This subspecies is an uncommon summer resident in the attenuated gallery forest, including wooded islands beyond the forest's contiguous distribution. There is a single

142

breeding record, a nest with two eggs in a small elm 0.2 m above the ground in a buckbrush thicket on 14 July along the upper north fork of Kings Creek. There are several observations of fledgling birds during July as well. There is one winter record for *P. e. erythrophthalmus*: 2 November 1983.

The wintering population arrives in early October and remains until early May; extreme dates are 21 September and 16 May. During October *P. e. maculatus* becomes common, but by November the transients have passed through, and this subspecies is uncommon throughout winter. It can be found along the edge of the gallery forest and attenuated gallery forest and occasionally in the rock outcrop community. During the winter of 1989–1990, following two years of drought, there were no towhees; the first transient appeared on 30 March, and it was *P. e. maculatus*.

American Tree Sparrow, *Spizella arborea* (Wilson)

Finck (1986) reported that this species is the most abundant winter resident on Konza Prairie, occurring in upland prairie, in the rock outcrop community, and along the edge of both the gallery forest and attenuated gallery forest (see also Figs. 14, 17, and 19). Tree sparrows arrive in late October; become especially numerous from December through February, when they occur in flocks of 75 to 100 birds; decrease in numbers during March; and are gone by early April in most years. Extreme dates are 15 October and 28 April. In winters following poor growing seasons, their tenure on Konza Prairie is truncated. For example, in the winter of 1988–1989 the last date of occurrence was 16 March.

Chipping Sparrow, *Spizella passerina* (Bechstein)

As Johnston (1964) pointed out, chipping sparrows are quite selective in their choice of conifers for nest sites in Kansas. It is for this reason that the chipping sparrow is not a summer resident on Konza Prairie. Yet it is a common transient, especially in spring when flocks of around 50 birds are frequently found feed-   143 ing in recently burned grassland sites or in elms setting seeds along the edge of the gallery forest. Dates of spring passage range from 8 April to 26 May. The chipping sparrow is uncommon in fall, occurring along the edge of the attenuated gallery forest, less frequently along the edge of the gallery forest, and in the rock outcrop community from 17 September to 29 October.

Clay-colored Sparrow, *Spizella pallida* (Swainson)

This species is an uncommon transient, usually found intermixed with flocks of chipping sparrows. Spring dates of passage range from 25 April to 16 May; fall dates are from 23 September to 5 October.

Field Sparrow, *Spizella pusilla* (Wilson)

First territorial songs of this species are heard in early March even while migrant flocks are passing through, and it remains a common resident until November along the edge of the attenuated gallery forest, in the rock outcrop community, and in prairie stream drainages containing small trees and patches of brush. Because of the field sparrow's dependence on woody vegetation, it does not occur in annually burned watersheds. This habitat selection is similar to that described by Kahl et al. (1985) for Missouri.

Relative abundances on June transects in unburned grassland sites average 2.83 ± 0.45 birds/km, intermediate between that in the attenuated gallery forest (5.16 ± 1.08 birds/km) and that for birds associated with the gallery forest (1.17 ± 0.32 birds/km). Although there is no difference between June populations in the attenuated forest and on unburned prairie, both of these means are significantly different from the small population along the edge of the gallery forest (Student's $t = 3.55$, df $= 18$, $P < 0.01$ for attenuated forest; Student's $t = 2.98$, df $= 18$, $P < 0.01$ for unburned prairie). The earliest breeding record is a nest with three eggs, 0.3 m above the ground in a 2.5-m elm sapling; it was found by Chris Smith on 21 May 1986. A late nest

144

with three eggs was found on 16 August 1991 in a plum thicket, 1.7 m off the ground, and adults have been observed still feeding fledglings as late as 2 September. The field sparrow is probably at least double brooded.

During the winter this species is uncommon, associating with the large flocks of tree sparrows in edge habitats. In some winters—for example, 1983–1984 and 1989–1990—field sparrows are absent.

Vesper Sparrow, *Pooecetes gramineus* (Gmelin)

This species is a common transient from late March to late April and again from mid-September until early November, with a few individuals lingering until mid-December (18 December 1982). Occasionally the vesper sparrow becomes abundant during the first two weeks of April as well as in early October. Extreme dates of record are 26 February to 28 April and 26 September to 10 November. It frequents grassland sites throughout the prairie as well as disturbed areas along the south fork of Kings Creek and is most readily seen in the shortgrass along Jeep trails and in the mowed fireguards.

Lark Sparrow, *Chondestes grammacus* (Say)

Lark sparrows occur as uncommon summer residents from mid-April to late August in areas of sparse grass cover, such as sites associated with poor soil and those disturbed by severe over-grazing as well as sites that are undergoing secondary succession following the abandonment of cropping. During periods of passage in April and September, the species often is common. Earliest arrival has been noted on 3 April, and the latest date is 8 October. Elmer Finck observed a pair copulating on 30 April 1986, and an adult accompanying "fluffy" plumaged juveniles on 13 June 1989 was seen by Melissa Brown. There are only two nest records. One nest was found on a gravelly piece of ground with sparse vegetation on 21 June 1991; the nest contained one

145

egg and one nestling. The other nest, discovered by Deb Beutler on 28 May 1992, contained four eggs.

Lark Bunting, *Calamospiza melanocorys* Stejneger

There are two records of this vagrant from western Kansas. Elmer Finck saw a female-plumaged bird on 28 September 1982 in the brome field north of N20A. On 2 June 1991 Jim Bennedix found a male along the old highway right-of-way in 2D.

Savannah Sparrow, *Passerculus sandwichensis* (Gmelin)

This sparrow is a common, occasionally abundant transient in grassland habitat from early March until mid-May and then again from late September to early November. There is one winter record (1 December 1982). Inclusive dates are 1 March to 18 May and 21 September to 11 November.

Grasshopper Sparrow, *Ammodramus savannarum* (Gmelin)

The grasshopper sparrow is an abundant summer resident in grassland habitats, being equally dense in unburned (8.28 ± 0.67 birds/km) and annually burned watersheds (6.84 ± 0.90 birds/km). Birds arrive in early April and remain until early October, although they are more difficult to find after the cessation of breeding in late August. Extreme dates of occurrence are 21 March to 29 October. There are 26 breeding records; nests with eggs have been found from 19 May to 17 July, and nests with young have been observed from 1 June to 6 July.

Henslow's Sparrow, *Ammodramus henslowii* (Audubon)

This enigmatic species is an uncommon summer resident that is restricted in its breeding habitat on Konza Prairie to unburned grasslands that have high densities of standing dead vegetation and low coverage by woody vegetation (Zimmerman 1988). Similarly, Peterson (1983) found Henslow's sparrows to frequent ungrazed pasture in which there was no woody vegetation. Kahl et al. (1985) demonstrated that this species also will not occur in overgrazed grasslands or those that have been recently mowed. The species will, however, occasionally invade spring-burned watersheds in late summer (E. Finck, personal communication; Skinner et al. 1984).

Birds arrive in mid-April and depart by the end of October, although they are difficult to detect once singing wanes in late summer. Extreme dates of occurrence are 5 April and 31 October. During the summer of 1974, Scott Hatch discovered three nests; one had five eggs on 22 June, another had one sparrow egg and one cowbird egg on 24 June, and a third had one sparrow egg, one cowbird egg, one sparrow young, and two cowbird young on 27 June. All other breeding evidence is indirect: an adult with nest material on 22 June 1983 and a bird carrying green caterpillars on 13 June 1984.

Le Conte's Sparrow, *Ammodramus leconteii* (Audubon)

During fall migration, this species is an uncommon transient from late September (27 September) through the second week in November (11 November), frequently being present in small flocks of 5 to 10 birds in prairie cordgrass swales, creek drainages with dogwood patches and small trees, and the rock outcrop community in upland prairie. In spring this species has never been observed in flocks and is only occasional in its occurrence during a relatively brief period from 30 March to 23 April.

Fox Sparrow, *Passerella iliaca* (Merrem)

The fox sparrow is an uncommon transient in March and April (extreme dates, 28 February to 13 April) and in fall from 4 October to 24 November. During both periods of passage it occurs along the edge of the gallery forest and in the attenuated gallery forest as well as in isolated patches of small trees and dogwood in upland prairie.

147

Song Sparrow, *Melospiza melodia* (Wilson)

This species is a common fall transient from late September through the end of November, becoming uncommon in the winter season and during spring migration. Inclusive dates are from 25 September to 8 May. During this period the song sparrow frequents the edges of the gallery forest and the attenuated gallery forest and occasionally can be found in brushy patches in upland prairie.

Lincoln's Sparrow, *Melospiza lincolnii* (Audubon)

This sparrow is a common transient from mid-March through mid-May; extreme dates are 12 March to 15 May and again from 14 September to 10 November. It is an occasional winter resident, with a few winter dates in the period from 21 December to 8 January. The Lincoln's sparrow occurs in habitats similar to those used by the song sparrow, but additionally it can be found in grassland sites in upland prairie far from extensive woody vegetation.

Swamp Sparrow, *Melospiza georgiana* (Latham)

The swamp sparrow is an uncommon transient associating with other sparrows in mixed-species flocks during spring from 28 March to 29 April and in autumn from 4 October to 4 November. There is one winter record for 22 February 1988.

White-throated Sparrow, *Zonotrichia albicollis* (Gmelin)

White-throats are uncommon transients during both vernal and autumnal periods of passage in mixed-species sparrow flocks in edge habitats. Spring dates range from 18 March to 12 May; in fall this species has been recorded from 30 September to 11 November.

White-crowns are uncommon transients from 25 April to 14 May and from 2 October through 17 November, but their numbers are less than those of the white-throated sparrow.

Harris' Sparrow, *Zonotrichia querula* (Nuttall)

Harris' sparrows are common transients in edge habitats from early March through May and again from mid-October to mid-December; they are uncommon to occasional during winter. Inclusive dates are 8 October to 31 May.

Dark-eyed Junco, *Junco hyemalis* (Linnaeus)

The junco arrives in October and is common throughout winter until its departure in April. Inclusive dates are 1 October to 25 April. *J. h. oreganus* is occasional within this period from early November until late March. In addition to occurring in edge habitats along with tree sparrows, juncos frequently can be found during winter feeding in shortgrass (mowed fireguards and areas around headquarters) and in cultivated fields.

Lapland Longspur, *Calcarius lapponicus* (Linnaeus)

Johnston (1965) considered this species a common transient and winter resident in Kansas grasslands, but in the tallgrass prairie of the Flint Hills Upland it is only occasional and typically only present in cultivated croplands or areas of shorter grasses. There are only two records for Konza Prairie: 20 December 1980 and 15 February 1984. Both sightings were along fireguards adjacent to upland prairie watersheds and involved no more than a dozen individuals.

Smith's Longspur, *Calcarius pictus* (Swainson)

This longspur is a rare transient in February, March, and November. Indeed, there are only three records. Two males were noted along the fireguard on the divide between K1B and C1A on 15 February 1984. During the next month, on 16 March 1984, Elmer

149

Finck found five birds in a weedy patch at the upper end of the
N4D watershed near the main trail. The third record was a single
bird flying over Campbell pasture on 7 November 1984.

Chestnut-collared Longspur, *Calcarius ornatus* (Townsend)

This species is a rare transient, having been recorded only twice
(17 March 1984 and 8 April 1986). Both records were single birds
on fireguards in upland prairie.

Snow Bunting, *Plectrophenax nivalis* (Linnaeus)

The snow bunting is a rare winter visitor. Two birds were seen by
Elmer Finck in a snow-free patch around the site of the old Cake-
house on 12 January 1984. The only other record was also obtained by Elmer Finck when a single bird was discovered in the
cultivated field along the main trail below headquarters on 5 November 1988.

Bobolink, *Dolichonyx oryzivorus* (Linnaeus)

There is one record for this species. Jan Knodel observed a single
individual in a grassland site along the middle fork of Swede
Creek on 12 June 1979.

Red-winged Blackbird, *Agelaius phoeniceus* (Linnaeus)

There are records for red-winged blackbirds in every week of the
year, but there is a definite pattern in this species' occurrence on
Konza Prairie. Red-wings are common summer residents in
marshy vegetation around ponds and seeps as well as along upland stream drainages where cattails also occur. Relative abundances on June transects in unburned watersheds average
1.62 ± 0.22 birds/km, whereas numbers on burned prairie equal
3.80 ± 0.37 birds/km. These means are significantly different
from each other (Student's $t = 5.06$, df $= 18$, $P < 0.01$), and this
difference reflects the presence of good cattail stands in watershed 1D.

The summer resident males arrive in April, followed in turn by the females in several weeks. Nest building is observed as early as 13 May, and nests with eggs have been found as late as 16 July. Fledged young are present by mid-June. In addition to being placed in cattails, nests are placed in sedge (*Caret* sp.) patches and in woody vegetation associated with stream drainages—dogwood, elm, elderberry, buckbrush, and cottonwood. By late August the breeding birds are gone, and the species becomes occasional until the third week in September, when it becomes common again as a result of the influx of migrant flocks. In some years these flocks are large (and include common grackles and cowbirds) and remain into winter, but usually these concentrations can no longer be found in upland prairie after early November. In most winters the species is occasional until the first migrant flocks appear in March.

Eastern Meadowlark, *Sturnella magna* (Linnaeus)

Eastern meadowlarks are the meadowlarks of the tallgrass prairie, occurring abundantly in upland prairie from early March until late November. The analysis by Kahl et al. (1985) reflected a similar choice in Missouri of grassland with sparse woody vegetation, dense ground cover, and some litter. Relative abundances during June surveys average 7.99 ± 0.41 birds/km in unburned prairie and 6.84 ± 0.80 birds/km on annually burned prairie. These means are not significantly different. During the winter months, however, the eastern meadowlark seldom occurs in upland prairie and is only occasional in brome fields and cultivated land adjacent to lower Kings Creek.

There are 35 nest records for Konza Prairie. Nests with eggs have been found from late April (22 April) until August (6 August). Recently fledged young have been seen as early as 28 May. It is not clear from these data or Johnston's (1964) account if the species is double brooded in Kansas.

151

Western Meadowlark, *Sturnella neglecta* Audubon

This occasional spring and summer visitor has been recorded from late February until mid-October. Singing birds have been observed, especially during March and April, in the disturbed area around the corral along the south fork of Kings Creek and more frequently along the edge of the cultivated fields adjacent to the headquarters entrance road and even occasionally in grassland watersheds. Nevertheless, the birds have never established territories.

Yellow-headed Blackbird, *Xanthocephalus xanthocephalus* (Bonaparte)

This species is an occasional transient in spring and fall. On 20 April 1990 a small flock was present in cattails on upper Pressee Branch. There is one fall record for 3 September 1982 of a single bird in the cultivated field along the headquarters entrance road.

Rusty Blackbird, *Euphagus carolinus* (Müller)

Dates of record for this occasional transient and winter visitor span the period from 7 November to 20 April, but it is irregular in its presence. During the 1982–1983 season it was regularly found in the attenuated forest and gallery forest, often associating with robins in dogwood patches. The following year (1983–1984) it again was present. But the only record since that time is of a single bird noted on 14 January 1987.

Brewer's Blackbird, *Euphagus cyanocephalus* (Wagler)

Almost all spring records of this uncommon April transient involve flocks (25 to 120 birds) feeding in recently burned watersheds in upland prairie. This species also is an occasional winter visitor.

Great-tailed Grackle, *Quiscalus mexicanus* (Gmelin)

After spreading into Kansas in 1964, the great-tailed grackle reached the Smoky Hill–Kansas river system in 1971 (Schwilling

1971) but was not discovered in the vicinity of Konza Prairie until five years later (Hansen 1983). There are only two records for this rare visitor to Konza Prairie: 13 May 1982 and 2 June 1987.

Common Grackle, *Quiscalus quiscula* (Linnaeus)

The grackle is a common summer resident. It arrives in late March and nests in the headquarters area and in trees associated with cattail swales in upper Pressee Branch and the middle fork of Swede Creek during May and early June. Foraging birds can regularly be found during summer in the gallery forest of Kings Creek. In September and October the common grackle becomes abundant as flocks numbering hundreds of birds visit forested sites and upland prairie. During November these flocks are smaller and less frequent, and by the end of the month grackles are gone from Konza Prairie. Inclusive dates are 16 March to 25 November. There is a single winter record on 18 December 1982.

Brown-headed Cowbird, *Molothrus ater* (Boddaert)

Cowbirds initially appear on Konza Prairie during March (earliest date, 4 March) and become common throughout the site in April and May. During June, July, and August they are abundant in upland prairie. Relative abundances in unburned prairie in June average 8.36 ± 0.51 birds/km, and the mean in annually burned prairie is 6.06 ± 1.24 birds/km. These means are not significantly different.

This brood parasite lays its eggs in nests of dickcissels, field sparrows, grasshopper sparrows, red-winged blackbirds, eastern meadowlarks, and Henslow's sparrows in prairie habitat as well as parasitizing nests of Bell's vireos, Louisiana waterthrushes, cardinals, and brown thrashers in the rock outcrop, attenuated gallery forest, and gallery forest communities. Farley (1987) found a cowbird egg in a Bewick's wren nest, but it was removed by the host. Cowbird eggs are also found in nests of phoebes, which utilize man-made structures on Konza Prairie.

Cowbird reproductive activity is intense during May and   153

June but decreases during July. Few host nests are parasitized by the third week in July (Zimmerman 1983). Cowbird populations on Konza Prairie abruptly decrease at the end of August, and the species is seldom seen after mid-November (latest date, 15 November in 1988). There are two winter dates, 1 December 1982 and 26 January 1987.

Orchard Oriole, *Icterus spurius* (Linnaeus)

This species is an uncommon summer resident from 4 May until early September, occurring along the edge of the attenuated gallery forest and in tree patches in upland prairie. It can regularly be observed foraging in grassland sites. There are two breeding records. Elmer Finck observed a female building in the cottonwoods by Westend Pond on 27 May 1982. The other record is of a nest with three eggs discovered 2.5 m up in a small elm on 9 June 1992.

Northern Oriole, *Icterus galbula* (Linnaeus)

This oriole is a common summer resident in the gallery forest and attenuated gallery forest, where relative abundances on June transects average 1.05 ± 0.48 birds/km and 0.15 ± 0.10 birds/km respectively. It is also observed in grassland sites and will nest in isolated cottonwoods; mean relative abundance in unburned prairie equals 0.43 ± 0.09 birds/km and 0.32 ± 0.10 birds/km in annually burned prairie. None of these means is significantly different from the others. Extreme dates of record are 1 May to 14 September. Pair formation and nest building begin soon after arrival (earliest date, 6 May) but continue throughout the month (latest date for building, 1 June). The species is single brooded in Kansas (Johnston 1964).

Purple Finch, *Carpodacus purpureus* (Gmelin)

The purple finch is an occasional winter visitor in the gallery forest and attenuated gallery forest during early November and in January and February.

House Finch, *Carpodacus mexicanus* (Müller)

Rapidly expanding populations of house finches from both western and eastern North America met in Kansas within the last few years (Podrebarac and Finck 1991). Although the species now regularly winters and breeds in the local area, there is only one record for Konza Prairie, a single bird discovered along the edge of the lower Kings Creek gallery forest on 9 November 1990.

Pine Siskin, *Carduelis pinus* (Wilson)

The siskin is an uncommon transient (March–April, October) and winter visitor (November–January). It is completely absent during some years (e.g., 1982–1983 and 1989–1990).

American Goldfinch, *Carduelis tristis* (Linnaeus)

Although this permanent resident becomes common in fall (September through November) if weed seed densities are high, it is usually uncommon along the edge of the gallery forest and in the attenuated gallery forest during the rest of the year. Breeding begins in June, with records for nest construction on 10 June and 30 June in dogwood thickets at the upper end of the attenuated gallery forest in both the south fork of Kings Creek and the Shane Creek drainage.

Evening Grosbeak, *Coccothraustes vespertinus* (Cooper)

The only records for this rare winter visitor were obtained by Marty and Sharon Gurtz when birds came to their feeder at the Hokansen house during December 1985.

House Sparrow, *Passer domesticus* (Linnaeus)

This uncommon permanent resident nests in association with man-made structures and is almost completely restricted to the headquarters area.

155

1 Phenological Checklist of the Birds of Konza Prairie

The following key defines the relative abundances indicated for each species (modified and updated from data previously published [Zimmerman 1985]).

• • • RARE. Very few records, not to be expected.

- - - - - OCCASIONAL. Irregular during the season indicated; or if regular, irregular in its annual frequency of occurrence.

——— UNCOMMON. Present during the season indicated at low densities. Appropriate habitats must be searched.

—— COMMON. Present in moderate densities during the seasons indicated and can be expected in appropriate habitats.

▬▬ ABUNDANT. Occurs at high densities, a very noticeable species in appropriate habitats.

Mar Apr May Jun Jul Aug Sep Oct Nov Dec Jan Feb

PIED-BILLED GREBE...
DOUBLE-CRESTED CORMORANT.................
AMERICAN BITTERN...............................
GREAT BLUE HERON................................
GREAT EGRET...
CATTLE EGRET.......................................
GREEN-BACKED HERON...........................
BLACK-CROWNED NIGHT-HERON.............
YELLOW-CROWNED NIGHT-HERON..........
WOOD DUCK..
GREEN-WINGED TEAL..............................
MALLARD..
BLUE-WINGED TEAL...............................
GADWALL..
AMERICAN WIGEON................................
RING-NECKED DUCK................................
COMMON GOLDENEYE............................
BUFFLEHEAD...
HOODED MERGANSER..............................
RUDDY DUCK..
TURKEY VULTURE...................................
OSPREY...
MISSISSIPPI KITE....................................
BALD EAGLE..
NORTHERN HARRIER................................
SHARP-SHINNED HAWK............................
COOPER'S HAWK.....................................
NORTHERN GOSHAWK..............................
BROAD-WINGED HAWK.............................
SWAINSON'S HAWK..................................
RED-TAILED HAWK...................................
ROUGH-LEGGED HAWK.............................
GOLDEN EAGLE.......................................
AMERICAN KESTREL.................................
MERLIN...
PEREGRINE FALCON.................................
PRAIRIE FALCON......................................
RING-NECKED PHEASANT...........................
GREATER PRAIRIE-CHICKEN.........................
WILD TURKEY..
NORTHERN BOBWHITE...............................
VIRGINIA RAIL..
SORA...
AMERICAN COOT.....................................
LESSER GOLDEN PLOVER............................
KILLDEER...
GREATER YELLOWLEGS..............................
LESSER YELLOWLEGS.................................
SOLITARY SANDPIPER................................
WILLET..
SPOTTED SANDPIPER................................
UPLAND SANDPIPER.................................

158

Species	Mar	Apr	May	Jun	Jul	Aug	Sep	Oct	Nov	Dec	Jan	Feb
MARBLED GODWIT												
LONG-BILLED DOWITCHER												
COMMON SNIPE												
AMERICAN WOODCOCK												
FRANKLIN'S GULL												
RING-BILLED GULL												
ROCK DOVE												
MOURNING DOVE												
BLACK-BILLED CUCKOO												
YELLOW-BILLED CUCKOO												
BARN OWL												
EASTERN SCREECH-OWL												
GREAT HORNED OWL												
BURROWING OWL												
BARRED OWL												
LONG-EARED OWL												
SHORT-EARED OWL												
COMMON NIGHTHAWK												
COMMON POORWILL												
CHUCK-WILL'S-WIDOW												
WHIP-POOR-WILL												
CHIMNEY SWIFT												
RUBY-THROATED HUMMINGBIRD												
BELTED KINGFISHER												
RED-HEADED WOOKPECKER												
RED-BELLIED WOODPECKER												
YELLOW-BELLIED SAPSUCKER												
DOWNY WOODPECKER												
HAIRY WOODPECKER												
NORTHERN FLICKER												
OLIVE-SIDED FLYCATCHER												
EASTERN WOOD-PEWEE												
WILLOW FLYCATCHER												
LEAST FLYCATCHER												
EASTERN PHOEBE												
GREAT CRESTED FLYCATCHER												
WESTERN KINGBIRD												
EASTERN KINGBIRD												
SCISSOR-TAILED FLYCATCHER												
HORNED LARK												
PURPLE MARTIN												
TREE SWALLOW												
NORTHERN ROUGH-WINGED SWALLOW												
CLIFF SWALLOW												
BARN SWALLOW												
BLUE JAY												
AMERICAN CROW												
BLACK-CAPPED CHICKADEE												
TUFTED TITMOUSE												
RED-BREASTED NUTHATCH												
WHITE-BREASTED NUTHATCH												
BROWN CREEPER												

159

Species	Mar	Apr	May	Jun	Jul	Aug	Sep	Oct	Nov	Dec	Jan	Feb
ROCK WREN								•				
CAROLINA WREN	▬	▬	▬	▬	▬	▬	▬	▬	▬	▬	▬	▬
BEWICK'S WREN	▬	▬	▬	▬	▬	▬	▬	-	-	-	-	-
HOUSE WREN	▬	▬	▬	▬	▬	▬	▬	-	-	-	-	-
WINTER WREN	-	-	-					-	-	-	-	-
SEDGE WREN		-	•									
MARSH WREN							•	•				
GOLDEN-CROWNED KINGLET	-	-	-					-	-	-	-	-
RUBY-CROWNED KINGLET	▬	▬	•				▬	▬	•			
BLUE-GRAY GNATCATCHER	▬	▬	▬	▬	▬	▬	▬					
EASTERN BLUEBIRD	▬	▬	▬	▬	▬	▬	▬	▬	▬	▬	▬	▬
MOUNTAIN BLUEBIRD	•									•		
VEERY		•										
GRAY-CHEEKED THRUSH		•										
SWAINSON'S THRUSH		▬	▬				-	-				
HERMIT THRUSH	▬	▬						-	-	-	▬	▬
WOOD THRUSH	▬	-	▬	▬	▬	▬	-	-				
AMERICAN ROBIN	▬	▬	▬	▬	▬	▬	▬	▬	▬	▬	▬	▬
GRAY CATBIRD	▬	▬	▬	▬	▬	▬	▬	▬				
NORTHERN MOCKINGBIRD	▬	-	-	-	-	-	-	-	•			
BROWN THRASHER	▬	▬	▬	▬	▬	▬	▬	▬				
AMERICAN PIPIT	-	-						-	-	-		
SPRAGUE'S PIPIT								•				
CEDAR WAXWING	▬	▬	▬						-	-	-	-
LOGGERHEAD SHRIKE	▬	▬	▬	▬	▬	▬	▬	▬	-	-	-	-
EUROPEAN STARLING	▬	▬	▬	▬	▬	▬	▬	▬	▬	▬	▬	▬
WHITE-EYED VIREO		•			-	-						
BELL'S VIREO			▬	▬	▬	▬	▬					
SOLITARY VIREO	-	-						▬				
WARBLING VIREO		▬	▬	▬	▬	▬	▬					
RED-EYED VIREO		▬	▬	▬	▬	▬	▬					
TENNESSEE WARBLER		▬	▬				▬					
ORANGE-CROWNED WARBLER	▬	▬					▬	▬				
NASHVILLE WARBLER		▬	▬				▬	▬				
NORTHERN PARULA	▬	-	-	-	-	-	-	-				
YELLOW WARBLER		▬	•				-	-				
CHESTNUT-SIDED WARBLER		•										
MAGNOLIA WARBLER		•						•				
YELLOW-RUMPED WARBLER	▬	▬						▬	▬	▬		
BLACK-THROATED GREEN WARBLER	-	-					-	-				
BLACKBURNIAN WARBLER	-	-										
PINE WARBLER	•	•										
PALM WARBLER								•	•			
BAY-BREASTED WARBLER							•					
BLACKPOLL WARBLER		▬	▬									
BLACK-AND-WHITE WARBLER	▬	▬	▬				▬	▬				
AMERICAN REDSTART		▬	▬				▬	▬				
OVENBIRD	-	-					•					
LOUISIANA WATERTHRUSH	▬	▬	▬	▬	▬	▬	-					
KENTUCKY WARBLER		-	-	-	-	-	-	-				
MOURNING WARBLER		-					-	-				
COMMON YELLOWTHROAT	.	▬	▬	▬	▬	▬	▬	▬				

	Mar Apr May Jun Jul Aug Sep Oct Nov Dec Jan Feb
WILSON'S WARBLER	
YELLOW-BREASTED CHAT	
SUMMER TANAGER	
SCARLET TANAGER	
NORTHERN CARDINAL	
ROSE-BREASTED GROSBEAK	
BLUE GROSBEAK	
LAZULI BUNTING	
INDIGO BUNTING	
DICKCISSEL	
RUFOUS-SIDED TOWHEE	
AMERICAN TREE SPARROW	
CHIPPING SPARROW	
CLAY-COLORED SPARROW	
FIELD SPARROW	
VESPER SPARROW	
LARK SPARROW	
LARK BUNTING	
SAVANNAH SPARROW	
GRASSHOPPER SPARROW	
HENSLOW'S SPARROW	
LECONTE'S SPARROW	
FOX SPARROW	
SONG SPARROW	
LINCOLN'S SPARROW	
SWAMP SPARROW	
WHITE-THROATED SPARROW	
WHITE-CROWNED SPARROW	
HARRIS' SPARROW	
DARK-EYED JUNCO	
LAPLAND LONGSPUR	
SMITH'S LONGSPUR	
CHESTNUT-COLLARED LONGSPUR	
SNOW BUNTING	
BOBOLINK	
RED-WINGED BLACKBIRD	
EASTERN MEADOWLARK	
WESTERN MEADOWLARK	
YELLOW-HEADED BLACKBIRD	
RUSTY BLACKBIRD	
BREWER'S BLACKBIRD	
GREAT-TAILED GRACKLE	
COMMON GRACKLE	
BROWN-HEADED COWBIRD	
ORCHARD ORIOLE	
NORTHERN ORIOLE	
PURPLE FINCH	
HOUSE FINCH	
PINE SISKIN	
AMERICAN GOLDFINCH	
EVENING GROSBEAK	
HOUSE SPARROW	

161

2   Vascular Plants
Mentioned in the Text
and Their Scientific Names

The names used in this list are based on Great Plains Flora Association (1986).

Cupressaceae, Cypress Family
Juniperus virginiana L. Red cedar

Platanaceae, Sycamore Family
Platanus occidentalis L. Sycamore

Ulmaceae, Elm Family
Celtis occidentalis L. Hackberry
Ulmus americana L. American elm

Moraceae, Mulberry Family
Maclura pomifera (Raf.) Schneid. Osage orange
Morus rubra L. Red mulberry

Juglandaceae, Walnut Family
Juglans nigra L. Black walnut

Fagaceae, Oak Family
Quercus macrocarpa Mischx. Bur oak
Quercus muehlenbergii Engelm. Chinquapin oak

163

Salicaceae, Willow Family
Populus deltoides Marsh. Cottonwood
Salix nigra Marsh. Black willow

Rosaceae, Rose Family
Prunus americana Marsh. American plum

Caesalpiniaceae, Caesalpinia Family
Cercis canadensis L. Eastern redbud
Gleditsia triacanthos L. Honey locust

Fabaceae, Legume Family
Amorpha canescens Pursh Lead plant
Amorpha fruticosa L. Indigobush

Cornaceae, Dogwood Family
Cornus drummondii C.A. Mey. Rough-leaved dogwood

Rhamnaceae, Buckthorn Family
Ceanothus herbaceous Raf. var. *pubescens* (T. & G.) New Jersey tea

Aceraceae, Maple Family
Acer negundo L. Box elder

Anacardiaceae, Cashew Family
Rhus aromatica Ait. var. *serotina* (Greene) Rehd. Aromatic sumac
Rhus glabra L. Smooth sumac
Toxicodendron radicans (L.) O. Ktze. Poison ivy

Rutaceae, Citrus Family
Zanthoxylum americanum P. Mill. Prickly ash

Verbenaceae, Vervain Family
Verbena stricta Vent. Hoary vervain

Lamiaceae, Mint Family
Salvia azurea Lam. Pitcher's sage

Oleaceae, Olive Family
164   *Fraxinus pennsylvanica* Marsh. Green ash

Caprifoliaceae, Honeysuckle Family

Sambucus canadensis L. Common elderberry
Symphoricarpos orbiculatus Moench. Buckbrush

Asteraceae, Sunflower Family

Ambrosia psilostachya DC. Western ragweed
Aster ericoides L. Heath aster
Grindelia squarrosa (Pursh) Dun. Curlycup gumweed
Vernonia baldwinii Torr. Inland ironweed

Poaceae, Grass Family

Andropogon gerardii Vitman Big bluestem
Andropogon scoparius Michx. Little bluestem
Bouteloua curtipendula (Michx.) Torr. Sideoats grama
Bouteloua gracilis (H.B.K.) Lag. ex Griffiths Blue grama
Bouteloua hirsuta Lag. Hairy grama
Bromus inermis Leyss. Smooth brome
Dichanthelium oligosanthes (Schult.) Gould var. *scriberianum* (Nash) Gould Scribner panicum
Elymus canadensis L. Canada wild rye
Festuca arundinacea Schreb. Tall fescue
Hordeum pusillum Nutt. Little barley
Koeleria pyramidata (Lam.) Beauv. Prairie junegrass
Panicum virgatum L. Switchgrass
Poa pratensis L. Kentucky bluegrass
Sorghastrum nutans (L.) Nash Indian grass
Spartina pectinata Link Prairie cordgrass
Sporobolus asper (Michx.) Kunth var. *asper* Tall dropseed

Typhaceae, Cattail Family

Typha latifolia L. Broad-leaved cattail

3   Glossary

BIOME A large geographic area affected by the same general climate and characterized over much of the region by a similar vegetative life form: e.g., deciduous forest, coniferous forest, grassland.

CLAYPAN Thin clay soils underlain by rock, presenting very xeric conditions.

COEFFICIENT OF VARIATION A measure of variability among a set of numerical values that is corrected for the mean value of the set so that it can then be compared to other similar sets of measurements whose mean value might be different.

CONTRANUPTIAL AREA The geographic area in which a bird occurs during the nonbreeding season.

ECOLOGICAL NICHE The sum total of all the environmental factors with which a species interacts and that affect its life and reproductive success. The niche includes both biotic (e.g., competitors, predators) and abiotic (e.g., temperature, soil conditions) factors.

ENDEMIC A group of organisms (usually a species) native to a particular area and found nowhere else.

EVAPOTRANSPIRATION The loss of water from plants that results from evaporation from their various above-ground parts as well as by transpiration through the pores (stomata) in the leaves.

FORB Any herbaceous (nonwoody) plant in the prairie that is not a grass.

GUILD A group of species that depend upon the same class of environmental resources and employ similar ways of exploiting them.

HABITAT SATURATION Habitat is the physical (structural) part of the environment that satisfies the needs of a species. It is the place the species lives, e.g., a forest, a pond, a prairie. The notion of habitat saturation suggests that the variety of species occurring in a particular habitat is utilizing the habitat to its fullest potential so that there is no opportunity for any other species to invade the habitat and meet its specific requirements. *See* resource partitioning.

167

INSECTIVORES Organisms that eat insects. Subcanopy insectivores gather their prey from the trees and shrubs that grow beneath the principal canopy of a forest. Sally insectivores gather their prey by flying out from an exposed perch and snatching the prey out of the air.

LEK A communal display area for the purpose of courtship and mating. Leks are typical not only of open-country grouse but are also used by some tundra shorebirds and several rain-forest perching birds.

LOESS Fine wind-blown soil that was deposited across the Great Plains, often to considerable depths, during the glacial period (Pleistocene). (Pronounced "luss.")

MERISTEMATIC TISSUE Undifferentiated parts of the plant in which cell division, hence growth, occurs.

MESIC A mid-point or moderate level in the gradient in soil moisture from saturated (hydric) to arid soils (xeric).

MYCORRHIZAL FUNGI A group of nonphotosynthetic organisms living in the soil but physically associated with the roots of plants. These symbiotic organisms facilitate the uptake of water and nutrients from the soil by the plants with which they are associated.

NICHE BREADTH The range of suitability of a particular environmental variable that is a component of a species' ecological niche.

OLDFIELD Cleared land or fallow agricultural land that is returning to a more stable community through the process of ecological succession.

PATCH-DEPENDENT The ecological landscape offers a variety of opportunities, often arrayed across the spatial dimensions of the habitat as discrete areas. Species requiring the particular resources associated with these areas have a distribution that is spatially dependent upon the distribution of these patches.

PHILOPATRY Literally, love of country; refers to the tendency of a bird to return to the same geographic area year after year, either to breed or to overwinter.

PINNAE Long, narrow neck feathers in several species of grouse that appear as "ears" when erected.

RELATIVE ABUNDANCE Absolute abundance is the number of objects in a particular area, like birds in an unburned watershed. Relative abundance is the number of objects per some common unit of measurement, such as a kilometer. Use of this parameter allows comparisons between two areas of different sizes in which absolute abundance will certainly differ but in which relative abundances could be similar.

RELATIVE DENSITY This measure is similar to relative abundance, except the common frame of reference is in terms of unit area, such as birds per hectare.

RESOURCE PARTITIONING A given resource, like weed seeds, may have a size distribution in the habitat. Or the distribution might be temporal, with some seeds being available in summer, others in fall. Different avian species avoid direct competition by the evolution of different adaptations to take advantage of some relatively discrete segment of a resource distribution. Thus birds with large bills are most efficient at taking large seeds, whereas birds with small bills are best adapted to feeding on small seeds.

SPECIES DIVERSITY A measure of abundance that takes into account the variety of species in an area as well as their relative densities.

SPECIES RICHNESS The number of different species in an area.

STOMATAL DENSITY The number of pores in a leaf per area of leaf surface. These pores, the stomata, are the openings through which gas exchange between the leaf tissue and the environment can be accomplished.

SUBSTRATE (VEGETATIVE) The plant community upon which a bird depends; most frequently connotes the physical structure provided by the plant community (see habitat saturation).

SYRINGEAL In birds the sound-producing organ is the syrinx, which is located at the base of the windpipe (trachea) as opposed to the arrangement in mammals where the sound-producing organ (larynx) is located at the top of the windpipe.

TAIGA The biome characterized by coniferous (cone-bearing) trees. It is best developed in the Northern Hemisphere, where it is circumpolar in distribution south of the tundra.

TALLGRASS Refers to the dominant grasses that thrive in mesic prairies: big bluestem, switchgrass, and Indian grass. These grasses begin their growing season coincident with the onset of summer rains and do not flower and set seed until late summer and early autumn. For this reason they are also referred to as warm-season grasses.

TERRITORY A defended area that is used to satisfy some particular (or all) resource needs of a species.

TILLERING The vegetative growth of grasses by which they send out stems (rhizomes) from the base of the plant and from which new above-ground stems develop.

TRANSECT A survey line across a habitat along which measurements are made. On Konza Prairie the transects for counting birds are oriented in an east-west direction so that the observer will have the sun at her (his) back when conducting the census in the early morning.

TROPHIC RESOURCE Food.

XERIC Soil conditions in which water content is the lowest on the continuum of soil moisture from hydric to mesic to xeric.

Literature Cited

Abrams, M. D. 1985. Fire history of oak gallery forest in a northeast Kansas tallgrass prairie. Amer. Midl. Nat. 114:188–191.

———. 1986. Historical development of gallery forest in northeast Kansas. Vegetatio 65:29–37.

———. 1988. Effects of prescribed fires on woody vegetation in a gallery forest understory in northeastern Kansas. Trans. Kansas Acad. Sci. 91:63–70.

Abrams, M. D., and L. C. Hulbert. 1987. Effect of topographic position and fire on species composition in tallgrass prairie in northeast Kansas. Amer. Midl. Nat. 117:442–445.

Abrams, M. D., A. K. Knapp, and L. C. Hulbert. 1986. A ten-year record of aboveground biomass in a Kansas tallgrass prairie: Effects of fire and topographic position. Amer. J. Bot. 73:1509–1515.

Anderson, R. C. 1990. The historic role of fire in the North American grassland. Pp. 8–18 in S. L. Collins and L. L. Wallace (eds.), Fire in North American tallgrass prairie. Univ. Oklahoma Press, Norman.

Ballard, W. B., Jr., and R. J. Robel. 1974. Reproductive importance of booming ground social organization in greater prairie chickens. Auk 91:75–85.

Barlow, J. C. 1962. Natural history of the Bell's vireo, *Vireo bellii* Audubon. Univ. Kansas Publ. Mus. Nat. Hist. 12:241–296.

Bentivenga, S. P., and B. A. D. Hetrick. 1991. Relationship between mycorrhizal activity, burning, and plant productivity in tallgrass prairie. Third Annual Konza Prairie LTER Workshop, 19 October 1991:4–5.

Blake, J. G. 1987. Species-area relationships of winter residents in isolated woodlots. Wilson Bull. 99:243–250.

Bock, C. E. 1987. Distribution-abundance relationships of some Arizona landbirds: A matter of scale. Ecology 68:124–129.

Bowen, D., Jr. 1971. A study of dummy nests and greater prairie chicken

LITERATURE CITED

(*Tympanuchus cupido pinnatus*) nests in northeastern Kansas with notes on female nesting behavior. M.S. Thesis. Kansas State Univ., Manhattan.

———. 1976. Coloniality, reproductive success, and habitat interactions in upland sandpipers (*Bartramia longicauda*). Ph.D. Thesis. Kansas State Univ., Manhattan.

Briggs, J. M., T. R. Seastedt, and D. J. Gibson. 1989. Comparative analysis of temporal and spatial variability in above-ground production in a deciduous forest and prairie. Holactic Ecol. 12:130–136.

Burnham, K. P., D. R. Anderson, and J. L. Laake. 1980. Estimation of density from line transect sampling of biological populations. Wildl. Monogr. 72:1–202.

Cody, M. L. 1966. The consistency of intra- and inter-continental grassland bird species counts. Amer. Nat. 100:371–376.

———. 1968. On the methods of resource division in grassland bird communities. Amer. Nat. 102:107–147.

———. 1985. Habitat selection in grassland and open-country birds. Pp. 193–226 in M. L. Cody (ed.), Habitat selection in birds. Academic Press, New York.

Collins, S. L., and D. J. Gibson. 1990. Effects of fire on community structure in tallgrass and mixed-grass prairie. Pp. 81–98 in S. L. Collins and L. L. Wallace (eds.), Fire in North American tallgrass prairies. Univ. Oklahoma Press, Norman.

Dale, B. C. 1984. Birds of grazed and ungrazed grasslands in Saskatchewan. Blue Jay 42:102–105.

Dixon, W. J., and F. J. Massey, Jr. 1957. Introduction to statistical analysis. 2d ed. McGraw-Hill, New York.

Dokken, D. A., and L. C. Hulbert. 1978. Effect of standing dead plants on stem density in bluestem prairie. Pp. 78–81 in D. C. Glenn-Lewin and R. Q. Landers, Jr. (eds.), Proc. 5th Midwest Prairie Conf. Iowa State Univ., Ames.

Elliott, P. F. 1980. Evolution of promiscuity in the brown-headed cowbird. Condor 82:138–141.

Evans, E. W. 1988a. Community dynamics of prairie grasshoppers subjected to period fire: Predictable trajectories or random walks in time? Oikos 52:283–292.

———. 1988b. Grasshopper (*Insecta:Orthoptera:Acrididae*) assemblages on tallgrass prairie: Influences of fire frequency, topography, and vegetation. Can. J. Zool. 66:1495–1501.

172

Faanes, C. A. 1984. Wooded islands in a sea of prairie. Amer. Birds 38: 3–6.

Fahnestock, J. T., and A. K. Knapp. 1991. Effects of bison herbivory on water relations and growth in tallgrass prairie forbs. Third Annual Konza Prairie LTER Workshop, 19 October 1991:9–10.

Farley, G. H. 1987. Comparative breeding strategies of two coexisting Passerines: Bell's vireo (*Vireo bellii*) and Bewick's wren (*Thryomanes bewickii*). M.S. Thesis. Kansas State Univ., Manhattan.

Finck, E. J. 1984a. Observation at a northern harrier nest. Kansas Ornithol. Soc. Bull. 35:24.

———. 1984b. Male dickcissel behavior in primary and secondary habitats. Wilson Bull. 96:672–680.

———. 1986. Birds wintering on the Konza Prairie Research Natural Area. Pp. 91–94 in G. K. Clambey and R. H. Pemble (eds.), Proc. 9th N. Amer. Prairie Conf. North Dakota State Univ., Fargo.

Fretwell, S. D. 1972. Populations in a seasonal environment. Princeton Univ. Press, Princeton, N.J.

Gibson, D. J. 1988. Regeneration and fluctuation of tallgrass prairie vegetation in response to burning frequency. Bull. Torrey Bot. Club 115:1–12.

———. 1989. Hulbert's study of factors effecting botanical composition of tallgrass prairie. Pp. 115–133 in T. B. Bragg and J. Stubbendieck (eds.), Proc. Eleventh N. Amer. Prairie Conf. Univ. Nebraska, Lincoln.

Gibson, D. J., and L. C. Hulbert. 1987. Effects of fire, topography and year-to-year climatic variation on species composition in tallgrass prairie. Vegetatio 72:175–185.

Gilliam, F. S., T. R. Seastedt, and A. K. Knapp. 1987. Canopy rainfall interception and throughfall in burned and unburned tallgrass prairie. Southwestern Nat. 32:267–271.

Gleason, H. A. 1939. The individualistic concept of the plant association. Amer. Midl. Nat. 21:92–110.

Gray, L. L. 1989. Correlations between insects and birds in tallgrass prairie riparian habitats. Pp. 263–265 in T. B. Bragg and J. Stubbendieck (eds.), Proc. Eleventh N. Amer. Prairie Conf. Univ. Nebraska, Lincoln.

Great Plains Flora Association. 1986. Flora of the Great Plains. T. M. Barkley (ed.), Univ. Press of Kansas, Lawrence.

Grubb, T. C., Jr., and L. Greenwald. 1982. Sparrows and a brushpile:

173

LITERATURE CITED

Foraging responses to different combinations of predation risk and energy cost. Anim. Behav. 30:637–640.

Grzybowski, J. A. 1982. Population structure in grassland bird communities during winter. Condor 84:137–152.

Hansen, S. C. 1983. Great-tailed grackle (*Quiscalus mexicanus*) range expansion and breeding biology in the central Great Plains. M.S. Thesis. Kansas State Univ., Manhattan.

Haukos, D. A., and G. S. Broda. 1989. Northern harrier (*Circus cyaneus*) predation of lesser prairie chicken (*Tympanuchus pallidicinctus*). J. Raptor Res. 23:182–183.

Hayes, D. C. 1985. Seasonal nitrogen translocation in big bluestem during drought conditions. J. Range Manage. 38:406–410.

Herbel, C. H., and K. L. Anderson. 1959. Response of true prairie vegetation on major Flint Hills range sites to grazing treatment. Ecol. Monogr. 29:171–186.

Hickey, M. B., and M. C. Brittingham. 1991. Population dynamics of blue jays at a bird feeder. Wilson Bull. 103:401–414.

Holmes, R. T., R. E. Bonney, and S. W. Pacala. 1979. Guild structure of the Hubbard Brook bird community: A multivariate approach. Ecology 60:512–520.

Holmes, R. T., and T. W. Sherry. 1988. Assessing population trends of New Hampshire forest birds: Local vs. regional patterns. Auk 105:756–768.

Horak, G. J. 1985. Kansas prairie chickens. Kansas Fish and Game Comm. Wildl. Bull. No. 3, v + 65 pp.

Hulbert, L. C. 1985. History and use of Konza Prairie Research Natural Area. Prairie Scout 5:63–93.

_____. 1986. Fire effects on tallgrass prairie. Pp. 138–142 in G. K. Clambey and R. H. Pemble (eds.), Proc. 9th N. Amer. Prairie Conf. North Dakota State Univ., Fargo.

_____. 1988. Causes of fire effects in tallgrass prairie. Ecology 69:46–58.

Jewett, J. M. 1941. The geology of Riley and Geary counties, Kansas. State Geol. Surv. Kansas Bull. 39.

Joern, A. 1986. Experimental study of avian predation on coexisting grasshopper populations (*Orthoptera:Acrididae*) in sandhills grasslands. Oikos 46:243–249.

Johnston, R. F. 1964. The breeding birds of Kansas. Univ. Kans. Publ. Mus. Nat. Hist. 12:575–655.

_____. 1965. A directory to the birds of Kansas. Univ. Kans. Mus. Nat. Hist. Miscell. Publ. 41:1–67.

Kahl, R. B., T. S. Baskett, J. A. Ellis, and J. N. Burroughs. 1985. Characteristics of summer habitat of selected nongame birds in Missouri. Univ. Missouri Agric. Exper. Sta. Bull. 1056:1–155.

Kantrud, H. A. 1981. Grazing intensity effects on the breeding avifauna of North Dakota native grassland. Can. Field-Nat. 95:404–417.

Kendeigh, S. C. 1941. Birds of a prairie community. Condor 43:165–174.

_____. 1982. Bird populations in east central Illinois: Fluctuations, variations, and development over a half-century. Illinois Biol. Monogr. 52:1–136.

Killingbeck, K. T. 1988. Microhabitat distribution of two *Quercus* (Fagaceae) species in relation to soil differences within a Kansas gallery forest. Southwestern Nat. 33:244–247.

Knapp, A. K. 1984a. Effect of fire in tallgrass prairie on seed production of *Veronia baldwinii* Torr. (Compositae). Southwestern Nat. 29:242–243.

_____. 1984b. Post-burn differences in solar radiation, leaf temperature and water stress influencing production in a lowland tallgrass prairie. Amer. J. Bot. 71:220–227.

_____. 1985. Effect of fire and drought on the ecophysiology of *Androgon gerardii* and *Panicum virgatum* in a tallgrass prairie. Ecology 66:1309–1320.

Knapp, A. K., and L. C. Hulbert. 1986. Production, density and height of flower stalks of three grasses in annually burned and unburned eastern Kansas tallgrass prairie: A four year record. Southwestern Nat. 31:235–241.

Knapp, A. K., and T. R. Seastedt. 1986. Detritus accumulation limits productivity of tallgrass prairie. BioScience 36:662–668.

Knight, C. 1991. Expansion of gallery forest between 1939 and 1985 on Konza Prairie Research Natural Area. Third Annual Konza Prairie LTER Workshop, 19 October 1991:19.

Knodel-Montz, J. 1981. Use of artificial perches on burned and unburned tallgrass prairie. Wilson Bull. 93:547–548.

Koelling, M. R., and C. L. Kucera. 1965. Dry matter losses and mineral leaching in bluestem standing crop and litter. Ecology 46:529–532.

Kucera, C. L., R. C. Dahlman, and M. R. Koelling. 1967. Total net productivity and turnover on an energy basis for tallgrass prairie. Ecology 48:536–541.

Lanyon, W. E. 1957. The comparative biology of the meadowlarks (*Sturnella*) in Wisconsin. Publ. Nuttall Ornithol. Club, No. 1, 67 pp.

Laurance, W. F., and E. Yensen. 1985. Rainfall and winter sparrow densities: A view from the northern Great Basin. Auk 102:152–158.

McArthur, J. V., M. E. Gurtz, C. M. Tate, and F. S. Gilliam. 1985. The interaction of biological and hydrological phenomena that mediate the qualities of water draining native tallgrass prairie on the Konza Prairie Research Natural Area. Pp. 478–482 in Perspectives on non-point source pollution. EPA 440/5-85-001.

Mengel, R. M. 1970. The North American central plains as an isolating agent in bird speciation. Pp. 279–340 in W. Dort, Jr., and J. K. Jones, Jr. (eds.), Pleistocene and recent environments of the Central Great Plains. Dept. Geology, Univ. Kansas Publ. 3.

Mikesell, F. 1988. Avian habitat selection in the attenuated riparian forest on the tallgrass prairie. M.S. Thesis. Kansas State Univ., Manhattan.

Orians, G. 1961. The ecology of blackbird (*Agelaius*) social systems. Ecol. Monogr. 31:285–312.

Peterson, A. 1983. Observations on habitat selection by Henslow's sparrows in Broome County, New York. Kingbird 33:155–164.

Podrebarac, D. K., and E. J. Finck. 1991. The winter distribution of the house finch in Kansas. Kans. Ornithol. Soc. Bull. 42:33–36.

Pulliam, H. R., and G. S. Mills. 1977. The use of space by wintering sparrows. Ecology 58:1393–1399.

Reichman, O. J. 1987. Konza Prairie, a tallgrass natural history. Univ. Press of Kansas, Lawrence.

Rhodes, R. 1991. The inland ground. Revised ed. Univ. Press of Kansas, Lawrence.

Risser, P. G., E. C. Birney, H. D. Blocker, S. W. May, W. J. Parton, and J. A. Wiens. 1981. The true prairie ecosystem. Hutchinson Ross Publ., Stroudsburg, Pa.

Robbins, C. S., J. R. Sauer, R. S. Greenberg, and S. Droege. 1989. Population declines in North American birds that migrate to the neotropics. Proc. Natl. Acad. Sci. 86:7658–7662.

Robel, R. J. 1964. Booming territory size and mating success of the greater prairie chicken (*Tympanuchus cupido pinnatus*). Anim. Behavior 14:328–331.

———. 1965. Quantitative indices to activity and territoriality of booming *Tympanuchus cupido pinnatus* in Kansas. Trans. Kansas Acad. Sci. 67:702–711.

———. 1970. Possible role of behavior in regulating greater prairie chicken populations. J. Wildl. Manage. 34:306–312.

Robel, R. J., J. N. Briggs, J. J. Cebula, N. J. Silvy, C. E. Viers, and P. G. Watt. 1970. Greater prairie chicken ranges, movements, and habitat usage in Kansas. J. Wildl. Manage. 34:286–306.

Robel, R. J., and W. B. Ballard, Jr. 1974. Lek social organization and reproductive success in the greater prairie chicken. Amer. Zool. 14:121–128.

Root, R. B. 1967. The niche exploitation pattern of the blue-gray gnatcatcher. Ecol. Monogr. 37:317–350.

Rotenberry, J. T., and J. A. Wiens. 1980. Habitat structure, patchiness, and avian communities in North American steppe vegetation: A multivariate analysis. Ecology 61:1228–1250.

Schartz, R. L., and J. L. Zimmerman. 1971. The time and energy budget of the male dickcissel (*Spiza americana*). Condor 73:65–76.

Schroeder, M. A., and C. E. Braun. 1992. Greater prairie-chicken attendance at leks and stability of leks in Colorado. Wilson Bull. 104:273–284.

Schwilling, M. D. 1971. Rapid increase and dispersal of boat-tailed grackles in Kansas. Kans. Ornithol. Soc. Bull. 22:15–16.

Seastedt, T. R. 1985. Canopy interception of nitrogen in bulk precipitation by annually burned and unburned tallgrass prairie. Oecologia 66:88–92.

Skinner, R. M., T. S. Baskett, and M. D. Blender. 1984. Bird habitats in Missouri prairies. Missouri Dept. Conserv. Terr. Ser. No. 14.

Smith, K. G. 1982. Drought-induced changes in avian community structure along a montane sere. Ecology 63:952–961.

———. 1986a. Winter population dynamics of red-headed woodpecker, blue jay, and northern mockingbird in the Ozarks. Amer. Midl. Nat. 115:52–62.

———. 1986b. Winter population dynamics of three species of mast-eating birds in the eastern United States. Wilson Bull. 98:407–418.

Smith, R. L. 1963. Some ecological notes on the grasshopper sparrow. Wilson Bull. 75:159–165.

———. 1968. Grasshopper sparrow. Pp. 725–745 in O. L. Austin, Jr. (ed.), Life histories of North American cardinals, grosbeaks, buntings, towhees, finches, sparrows, and allies. U.S. Natl. Museum Bull. 237, part 2.

Thompson, M., and C. Ely. 1989. Birds in Kansas. Vol. I. Univ. Kansas Mus. Nat. Hist. Publ. Education Ser. No. 11.

LITERATURE CITED

Vinton, M. A., and D. C. Hartnett. 1992. Effects of bison grazing on *Andropogon gerardii* and *Panicum virgatum* in burned and unburned tallgrass prairie. Oecologia 90:374–382.

Vinton, M. A., D. C. Hartnett, E. J. Finck, and J. M. Briggs. In press. Bison (*Bison bison*) grazing patterns and interactions with fire on a Kansas tallgrass prairie. Amer. Midl. Nat.

Ward, L. E., R. Kazmaier, and D. C. Hartnett. 1991. Forb species response to bison activity on Kansas tallgrass prairie. Third Annual Konza Prairie LTER Workshop, 19 October 1991:27.

Weaver, J. E. 1954. North American prairie. Johnsen Publ. Co., Lincoln, Nebr.

Weaver, J. E., and N. W. Rowland. 1952. Effects of excessive natural mulch on development, yield, and structure of native grassland. Bot. Gaz. 114:1–19.

Wells, P. V. 1970. Historical factors controlling vegetation patterns and floristic distributions in the central plains region of North America. Pp. 211–240 in W. Dort, Jr., and J. K. Jones, Jr. (eds.), Pleistocene and recent environments of the Central Great Plains. Dept. Geology, Univ. Kansas Publ. 3.

Whittaker, R. H. 1951. A criticism of the plant association and climatic climax concepts. Northwest Sci. 25:17–31.

Wiens, J. A. 1969. An approach to the study of ecological relationships among grassland birds. Ornithol. Monogr. 8:1–93.

———. 1973. Pattern and process in grassland bird communities. Ecol. Monogr. 43:237–270.

———. 1974. Climatic instability and the "ecological saturation" of bird communities in North American grasslands. Condor 76:385–400.

———. 1975. Avian communities, energetics, and functions in coniferous forest habitats. Proc. Symp. Management of Forest and Range Habitats for Nongame Birds, USDA Forest Service Gen. Tech. Rept. WO-1:226–265.

———. 1976. Population responses to patchy environments. Ann. Rev. Ecol. Syst. 7:81–120.

Wiens, J. A., and M. I. Dyer. 1975. Rangeland avifaunas: Their composition, energetics, and role in the ecosystem. Proc. Symp. Management of Forest and Range Habitats for Nongame Birds, USDA Forest Service Gen. Tech. Rept. WO-1:146–182.

Williams, J. B., and G. O. Batzli. 1979. Competition among bark-foraging birds in central Illinois: Experimental evidence. Condor 81:122–132.

Willson, M. F. 1974. Avian community organization and habitat structure. Ecology 55:1017–1029.

Zimmerman, J. L. 1966. Polygyny in the dickcissel. Auk 83:534–546.

_____. 1971. The territory and its density dependent effect in *Spiza americana*. Auk 88:591–612.

_____. 1983. Cowbird parasitism of dickcissels in different habitats and at different nest densities. Wilson Bull. 95:7–22.

_____. 1984. Nest predation and its relationship to habitat and nest density in dickcissels. Condor 86:68–72.

_____. 1985. The birds of Konza Prairie Research Natural Area, Kansas. Prairie Nat. 17:185–192.

_____. 1988. Breeding season habitat selection by the Henslow's sparrow (*Ammodramus henslowii*) in Kansas. Wilson Bull. 100:17–24.

_____. 1992. Density-independent factors affecting the avian diversity of the tallgrass prairie community. Wilson Bull. 104:85–94.

Zimmerman, J. L., and E. J. Finck. 1989. Philopatry and correlates of territorial fidelity in male dickcissels. N. Amer. Bird Bander 14:83–85.

Index